THE BEST OF
Christopher Idone

THE BEST OF
Christopher Idone

STEWART, TABORI & CHANG

NEW YORK

Text and recipes copyright © 1997 Christopher Idone

Photographs are copyrighted as follows:
Pages 2–3, 7, 8–9, 10, 11 (right and bottom), 20, 22, 25, 28, 29, 30, 31, 38–39, 40, 46, 55, 65, 66, 69, 76–77, 79, 80, 87, 88, 91, 92, 96–97, 99, 102, 105, 106, 110, 123 (bottom), 128, and endpapers © 1997 Christopher Idone
Pages 11 top left, 12–13, 16, 24, 34, 35. 43, 44, 58, 61, 62, 93, 94, 109, 113, 114, 118, 122, © 1997 Tom Eckerle
Pages 15, 32, 48, 51, 70, 72, 82, 84, 123 (top) © 1997 Richard Jeffrey
Pages 37, 86, 116 © 1997 Rico Puhlmann
Page 120 © 1997 Todd Weinstein

Published in 1997 and distributed in the U.S. by
Stewart, Tabori & Chang, a division of U.S. Media Holdings, Inc.
575 Broadway, New York, New York 10012

Distributed in Canada by General Publishing Co. Ltd.
30 Lesmill Road, Don Mills, Ontario, Canada M3B 2T6
Distributed in Australia by Peribo Pty Ltd.
58 Beaumont Road, Mount Kuring-gai, NSW 2080, Australia
Distributed in all other territories by Grantham Book Services Ltd.
Isaac Newton Way, Alma Park Industrial Estate, Grantham,
Lincolnshire, NG31 9SD England

Library of Congress Cataloging-in-Publication Data:

Idone, Christopher.
        The best of Christopher Idone.
            p.   cm.
        ISBN 1-55670-553-0
        I. Cookery.   I. Title.
    TX714.II5   1996
    641.5—dc21   96-36965

Edited by Linda Sunshine and Mary Kalamaras
Designed by Melanie Random

Front cover: Bruschetta with Fresh Tomatoes (Recipe page 23)
Back cover: Peas and Mint Leaves

Printed in Singapore

10 9 8 7 6 5 4 3 2 1

Foreword

...

I am at the stage in my life when the time I spend cooking in the kitchen must be fun. I don't want to impress my friends; just serve a good meal, make them happy, have good conversation, and kiss them goodbye when it's time for them to leave.

I remain true to myself which means being true to the season. I lust for the first shad roe of spring and the sorrels and morels that come with it. Later, I want asparagus and young lamb followed by sweet soft-shell crabs, and strawberries, mostly with short-cake and whipped cream. I can patiently wait for the first just-picked tender corn and vine-ripened tomatoes in summer. And in winter I want my kitchen to smell of roasting smoked hams, roasts, and stews; and collect apples of every kind to turn into tarts, sauces, and compotes. I'll serve roasted chicken and mashed potatoes almost anytime, and pasta in any form in between.

Seasons are brief: I won't buy peaches in November or asparagus in December, and the winter tomato is never a substitute, no matter what they say. I'd rather use canned.

I want shopping to be easy, but I'll make a detour for the best peaches or berries, only when necessary, and that's just because I know where to find them. Most of the time I find everything I want from the few good markets I have been shopping from for years. I'm particular and quirky about one thing only. And that's fish. I have one purveyor in the entire city of New York and another at the east end of Long Island. And if I can't get it, I do without. By that, I mean I change the menu.

I remember what my friends like, their favorite dishes and petty dislikes. I sometimes repeat dishes that they like more than I do because it gives me pleasure seeing them content and satisfied. I get requests from some for recipes that are printed in books I have written: they have either misplaced them, given them away, or are too lazy to read the text. It's a form of flattery to be sure, but while talking out a recipe over the phone, I will usually change it—just because cooking styles change and repetition is boring. But then, certain things remain terrific, and why change them if they are good? I am stimulated by the cooking of others and enjoy cooking their recipes, too. After all, cooking as well as eating is all about sharing, and recipes are reinvented all the time.

I have not lost my zest for cooking and feeding people, but I have learned to make it simpler. I used to love pickling and putting up relishes in the fall. Now I take short cuts and prepare little batches that will keep for a couple of weeks in the refrigerator. When I do "production," it is only with the help of friends. There is something daunting when facing a bushel of cucumbers or corn on your own, but it becomes playful and merry-making when performing the task with a bunch of pals, even though they leave with most of the spoils anyway.

I used to make dozens of fruitcakes in early fall, soaking them in brandy and sending them off at Christmas. But it took years to realize they were often passed along. (One actually came back to me.) No, we don't eat fruitcake anymore. And I don't spend days in the kitchen cooking the annual cassoulet or rendering a goose and turning it into confit. Braised lamb shanks and a pot of seasoned white beans satisfy that hankering and it takes a fifth of the time.

I have friends who are better eaters than cooks and I hold them in as much esteem as my friends who can cook. Both, I think, are the most essential ingredients to a meal. Gathering at the table is the most felicitous part of our daily lives, and though every dinner is not a dinner party, whatever we serve should be prepared with thoughtfulness and the desire to please. And though it isn't true that if you can light a match and boil water you can cook, it doesn't

require a magician either. Good cooking requires quality ingredients and a little know-how around the kitchen. A battery of utensils is of little help. What you need are a few good pots, a couple of nicely weighted sharp knives, a vegetable peeler, a potato masher, a blender or cuisinart if you like to purée things, some bowls, and some nice platters and plates to serve the food you cook.

Fewer people are intimidated by cooking today. They have a particular repertoire that serves them well. The good ones discover and branch out. They invite you to dinner, give you a good time, and that's it. And that's what entertaining has always been and will always be.

The recipes that follow are a capsulated version of the things I like to cook and the dishes that are particularly pleasing to my friends. No, not every recipe I prepare is a showstopper, but every recipe is for an occasion. And I hope you will turn these recipes into meals that will celebrate your occasions.

—February, 1997

Table of Contents

Appetizers

...

Artichokes Benedict 14

Puff Pastry with Asparagus and Mushrooms 17

Littlenecks with Herb Butter 18

Steamed Mussel and Potato Salad 21

Cannellini Beans and Tuna 23

Bruschetta with Fresh Tomatoes 23

Cold Oysters and Lamb Sausage 24

Country Salad 25

Celery-Root Remoulade 26

Succotash and Lobster 27

Summer Salad 29

Caprese Salad 30

Papaya with Shrimp and Yogurt-Dill Dressing 31

Pistou: Mediterranean Vegetable Soup with Basil Sauce 32

Black Bean Soup 34

Purée of Pea Soup with Mint 35

Fish Soup with Rouille 36

Main Courses

...

Red Scallop Pasta 41

Pasta with Clams, Mussels, and Sausage 42

Lemon Risotto 45

Stewed Apples with Macaroni and Cheese 46

Chicken Pot Pie 49

Roast Chicken 50

Osso Buco 51

Braised Lamb Shanks with White Beans 52

Lamb Stew 53

Steak Salad with Vegetables 54

Meatloaf 56

Choucroute 57

Shepherd's Pie 59

Marinated Grilled Salmon 60

Grilled Swordfish with Salt Crust and
Gin-Lime Butter 63

Moqueca: Bahia Fish Stew 64

Pumpkin Baked with Creamed Shrimp, Rio Style 67

Crab and Salmon Cakes 68

Bourride with Aïoli 71

Salad Niçoise 73

Grilled Duck Breast Salad 74

About Making Stock 75

Vegetables and Condiments

...

Wild Mushroom Bread Pudding 78

Moroccan Eggplant with Tahini Yogurt 80

Herbed Mashed Potatoes with Roquefort Cheese 81

Corn Soufflé 82

Ratatouille 85

Grilled Corn 86

Pickled Herring 87

Hot Hot Tomato Chutney 89

Onion Marmalade 90

Tapenade: Olive Paste 92

Pickled Pears 93

Plum Ketchup 95

Spiced Peaches 95

Desserts and Drinks

...

Orange Brulée 98

Chocolate-Brittle Ice Cream 100

Cherry Clafouti 101

Roasted Pineapple Caribe 103

Spiced Poached Figs with Pinot Noir Syrup 104

Lemon Curd Tartlets 107

Coconut Flan 108

Ovos Nevados 111

Lemon Cake 112

Berry Shortcake 115

Plum Tart 116

Bread Pudding Soufflé with Whiskey Sauce 117

Tropical Fruit Sorbet 119

Blueberry Breakfast Muffins 120

Lemonade 123

Moroccan Mint Tea 123

Index 126

Appetizers

Artichokes Benedict

...

¹/₄ cup all-purpose flour
¹/₄ cup fresh lemon juice
4 large artichokes
1 lemon, halved
4 medium carrots, peeled and chopped
Salt and freshly ground white pepper, to taste

FOR THE BEURRE BLANC
¹/₂ cup fresh orange juice, preferably from a blood or navel orange
¹/₂ cup dry white wine
10 tablespoons unsalted butter, chilled and cut into small pieces
1 tablespoon tarragon white-wine vinegar
4 eggs
1 tablespoon chopped fresh chives

In a medium bowl, whisk the flour and lemon juice together to make a paste, then whisk in 6 cups cold water. One at a time, cut away the stems of the artichokes and rub each bottom with a lemon half. Remove and discard the tough outer leaves until those exposed are folded inward and are creamy green in color. Cut off the cone of leaves halfway down from the top and discard. Rub the cut surface with the used lemon half and drop into the water-flour mixture.

Fill a large nonreactive pot with lightly salted water and bring to a boil. Squeeze the remaining lemon half into the boiling water. Add the drained artichokes, reduce the heat, and simmer about 30 minutes until the bottoms are tender and can be easily pierced with a sharp paring knife. Remove the artichoke bottoms with a slotted spoon to a colander, cool under cold running water, and drain. (The hearts can be prepared one day ahead: prepare up to this point, cover, and refrigerate.)

Carefully remove the remaining leaves, disturbing the bottom as little as possible. Scrape out the choke with the tip of a spoon. Trim the sides to make a neat shape. Shave the bottoms flat so they will sit level. Cover and keep warm, or reheat in a steamer over boiling water.

In a medium saucepan of lightly salted boiling water, cook the carrots until tender, about 6 to 8 minutes. Drain, and purée in a food processor. Season with salt and pepper and keep warm in a double boiler over simmering water.

Prepare the beurre blanc: In a nonreactive medium saucepan, boil the orange juice and white wine over medium heat until the liquid is syrupy and reduced by two-thirds, about 12 minutes.

Remove the pan from the heat and whisk in 2 tablespoons of the butter, one piece at a time. Return to low heat and, whisking constantly, add the remaining butter, one piece at a time. When all of the butter is added, the sauce will have the creamy smooth consistency of a hollandaise. Remove the pan to the warm side of the stove to keep warm.

Bring a large saucepan of water to a simmer. Add the vinegar. One at a time, carefully break each egg into the water. Using a large spoon, quickly lift the setting white around each egg and spoon it towards the egg yolk to help the eggs poach into oval shapes. Simmer gently until the whites are firm, but the yolks are still soft, about 4 minutes. Use a slotted spoon to transfer the eggs to paper toweling to drain briefly. Trim away some of the whites so the eggs will sit neatly on top of the artichoke hearts. Set the cooked poached eggs aside in a bowl of ice water until ready to serve, up to 2 hours. (You should have extra eggs on hand just in case any should break.)

Bring a skillet of plain water to a simmer. With a slotted spoon, transfer the poached eggs to the water and heat through, about 2 minutes. Place the artichoke hearts on individual warm plates and fill the wells with a spoonful of the carrot purée. Use the slotted spoon to place the eggs on top of the purée. Spoon the beurre blanc over the eggs and sprinkle with chives.

Puff Pastry with Asparagus and Mushrooms

...

SERVES 4

$^1/_2$ pound homemade puff pastry, or 1 defrosted frozen puff pastry
  sheet (see Note)

1 egg yolk

2 tablespoons unsalted butter

$^3/_4$ pound medium mushrooms (preferably cremini), sliced
  $^1/_8$-inch thick

Salt and freshly ground black pepper, to taste

16 to 24 asparagus stalks, trimmed and peeled into 6-inch spears

FOR THE SAUCE

$^1/_2$ cup dry white wine

$^1/_2$ cup fresh orange juice

1 tablespoon raspberry or other fruit-flavored vinegar

12 tablespoons (1$^1/_2$ sticks) unsalted butter, chilled and cut into bits

1 tablespoon meat or chicken demi-glace (optional)

Preheat the oven to 375°F. Line a 12 x 18-inch baking sheet with parchment paper and sprinkle with water.

On a lightly floured surface, roll out the pastry into a 14 x 5-inch rectangle $^1/_8$-inch thick. Cut the pastry into 4 rectangles. Place them on the prepared sheet about 1$^1/_2$ inches apart to allow for expansion during baking. Cover with plastic wrap and refrigerate for 20 minutes, or until chilled.

Beat the egg yolk with 2 tablespoons cold water. Brush the tops of the chilled pastry lightly with the egg wash. Bake for 20 minutes, or until puffed and golden.

Meanwhile, in a large skillet, melt the butter over medium heat. Add the mushrooms and season with salt and pepper. Cook, stirring from time to time, just until the mushrooms give off their liquid, about 5 minutes. Pour off the cooking liquid into a saucepan. Keep the mushrooms warm. Cook the liquid over low heat until reduced to about 1 tablespoon. Set aside.

In a medium saucepan of lightly salted simmering water, poach the asparagus for 5 to 7 minutes, or until crisp-tender. Drain and keep warm.

Prepare the sauce: Place the wine, orange juice, and vinegar in a small nonreactive heavy saucepan over medium heat and slowly bring to a simmer. Continue to simmer until the mixture is syrupy and reduced to about 2 tablespoons. Remove the pan from the heat and whisk in about 2 tablespoons of the butter pieces. Return to low heat, and whisking constantly, add the remaining butter piece by piece. Whisk in the reduced mushroom liquid and optional demi-glace. Set aside on the warm side of the stove.

Using a serrated knife, carefully slice each pastry in half lengthwise. Place each bottom slice on an individual warm plate. Divide the mushrooms over each, then add the asparagus spears. Coat the asparagus with the sauce. Place the top pastry over the asparagus and serve immediately.

Note: Excellent quality frozen puff pastry is available at specialty food stores and supermarkets.

Littlenecks with Herb Butter

...

Approximately 12 small littleneck clams per person, well-scrubbed

FOR THE SAUCE
1 cup melted butter
2 garlic cloves, minced

2 tablespoons minced parsley
1 tablespoon chopped tarragon leaves
1 tablespoon chopped chives
Freshly ground black pepper, to taste

Place the clams in the freezer for 10 minutes before cooking.

Prepare the sauce: In a small saucepan, bring the butter to a simmer over medium-low heat. Pour into a glass measuring cup and let stand 5 minutes. Skim off and discard the foam on top. Pour the clarified butter into a bowl, discarding the milky residue. Add the garlic, parsley, tarragon, and chives. Season with pepper to taste and set aside.

In a large covered steamer kettle, bring 1 cup cold water to a rolling boil over high heat. Place the clams in the steamer basket, cover, and cook the clams just until they open. (Peek in after about 4 minutes.) Using tongs or a slotted spoon, begin transferring the open clams to a large bowl. Discard any that do not open.

Strain the clam juice through a fine sieve into the butter mixture, leaving any sand in the bottom of the kettle; heat slightly. Season with the pepper. Divide the clams evenly among warm soup bowls and cover with sauce.

To grill the clams: Prepare a charcoal fire. When the coals are dusty and glowing, place the clams on the grill. As they open, use long tongs to transfer them to a large bowl. Use the clam juice that collects in the bottom of the bowl to make the sauce.

Steamed Mussel and Potato Salad

...

SERVES 4–5

4 quarts mussels, scrubbed and debearded
2 cups dry white wine or water
4 large Idaho or russet potatoes
4 scallions, chopped (include some of the green)
1/4 cup olive oil

3 tablespoons tarragon white-wine vinegar
Salt and freshly ground black pepper, to taste
1 small black truffle, thinly sliced and julienned (optional)

Place the mussels in the freezer for 10 minutes before steaming.

In a large covered steam kettle, bring the wine to a rolling boil over high heat. Place the mussels in the steam basket, cover, and cook just until they open. (Peek in after about 4 minutes.) Using tongs or a slotted spoon, begin transferring the open mussels to a large bowl. Discard any mussels that do not open.

Strain the cooking liquid through a wire strainer lined with a double thickness of cheesecloth, and reserve. With a sharp paring knife, remove the mussels from the shells and reserve them in the strained juice.

In a large saucepan of lightly salted boiling water, cook the potatoes until tender when pierced with a knife, about 20 minutes. Drain and rinse under cold running water until cool enough to handle. Peel, cut into quarters lengthwise, then thinly slice. Place the potato slices in a large bowl. Add the scallions.

Lift the mussels out of the liquid and add to the potatoes. In a small bowl, whisk the oil and vinegar, pour over the potatoes and toss. Add just enough of the mussel cooking liquid to moisten as desired. Season with salt and pepper. Serve chilled or at room temperature, sprinkled with the optional truffle.

Note: The steamed mussels are also delicious on their own. Add 1 cup of minced onion, 1 minced garlic clove, and a few fresh parsley sprigs to the wine before steaming the mussels. Mix 1/2 cup chopped parsley into the strained juice, pour over the hot mussels, and serve.

Cannellini Beans and Tuna

2 cups (1 pound) dried cannellini (white kidney) or Great Northern beans
1 small onion, peeled and halved
2 whole cloves
3 garlic cloves, crushed
1 sprig fresh thyme
1 sprig fresh sage

Salt and freshly ground black pepper, to taste
1 teaspoon crushed red-pepper flakes
$1/4$ cup olive oil, or to taste
1 (6-ounce) can Italian-style tuna fish packed in oil, drained and flaked
$1/4$ cup chopped fresh parsley

Rinse the beans and place in a bowl of cold water to cover. Set aside for 4 hours or overnight.

Preheat the oven to 275°F. Drain the beans and place them in an flameproof casserole. Stud the onion halves with the whole cloves and bury them in the casserole with the garlic, thyme, and sage. Add enough cold water to cover by $1/2$ inch and cover. Place casserole over low heat and bring contents to a simmer. Remove from the heat and place in oven. Bake until the beans are tender but not mushy, about 45 minutes. (Check after 15 minutes to be sure that the liquid is simmering and is still above the level of the beans, adding boiling water if necessary.) Season with the salt, pepper, and pepper flakes. Set aside, uncovered, until cooled. Cover and refrigerate until chilled.

When ready to serve, remove the onion, garlic, and herbs. Fold in the oil and drained tuna. Serve at room temperature, sprinkled with parsley.

Note: The beans are also a great topping for bruschetta.

Bruschetta with Fresh Tomatoes

MAKES 4 BRUSCHETTA

2 large ripe tomatoes, cored and chopped
1 tablespoon olive oil, plus additional for serving
1 teaspoon balsamic vinegar
$1/2$ teaspoon chopped fresh marjoram leaves

Salt and freshly ground black pepper, to taste
4 large slices crusty hearth-baked country bread, sliced about 6 inches long and 1-inch thick
8 fresh basil leaves, cut into thin strips

In a bowl, combine the tomatoes, olive oil, vinegar and marjoram leaves, and season with salt and pepper. Set aside for 10 minutes to allow the tomatoes to release some of their juices.

Grill or toast the bread on both sides.

Place the grilled bread on individual plates and spoon the tomato mixture on top. Sprinkle with the basil and serve with extra olive oil for drizzling.

Cold Oysters and Lamb Sausage

...

FOR THE PATTIES

1 pound lean lamb, ground twice

1/3 pound pork fat, ground twice

1 glarlic clove, minced

2 tablespoons chopped fresh parsley

2 teaspoons chopped fresh sage

1/2 teaspoon chopped fresh rosemary

3/4 teaspoon salt

1/2 teaspoon coarsely ground black pepper

2 tablespoons unsalted butter

4 to 6 oysters per person, freshly shucked

In a mixing bowl, combine the lamb and pork fat with the garlic, parsley, sage, rosemary, salt, and pepper and mix well.

Using about 1/4 cup of mixture for each patty, shape into 12 small round patties about 3/4-inch thick. Melt the butter in a large skillet over medium-high heat. Add the sausage patties and reduce the heat to medium. Brown the patties evenly on both sides for about 5 minutes, turning once. The patties should be served medium rare.

Place on paper toweling and pat dry. Serve immediately with the raw oysters.

Country Salad

FOR THE SALAD

1 large head white chicory (frisée) washed
*   and dried*
1 large ripe pear
1 tablespoon fresh lemon juice
8 ounces slab bacon, sliced $^1/_3$-inch thick
*   and then into $^1/_2$-inch pieces*
1 cup walnut halves

FOR THE DRESSING

Salt, to taste
3 tablespoons white-wine vinegar
1 tablespoon Dijon mustard
Freshly ground black pepper, to taste
$^1/_4$ cup olive oil
8 ounces Roquefort cheese, crumbled

Tear the chicory into bite-size pieces. Place in a large salad bowl, cover with paper toweling, and refrigerate.

Peel the pear and cut into $^1/_2$-inch cubes. Place the cubes in a small bowl and toss with the lemon juice. Set aside.

In a small skillet over medium heat, cook the bacon until crisp and golden, about 5 minutes. Drain the bacon on paper toweling. Discard the bacon fat and wipe off the skillet. Add the walnuts to the skillet and toast over low heat, stirring often, just until they begin to give off their oil, about 2 min-utes. Remove from the heat and set aside.

Prepare the dressing: In a small bowl, whisk the salt, vine-gar, and mustard with the pepper. Gradually add the oil and whisk until emulsified. Set aside.

Pour the dressing over the chicory and toss to coat. Divide the salad among 4 plates and sprinkle with the bacon, pear, walnuts, and Roquefort cheese.

Celery-Root Remoulade

...

2 large celery roots (celeriac), about 1 pound

2 teaspoons fresh lemon juice

Salt, to taste

1 large tart green apple (such as pippin or Granny Smith), peeled and cored

FOR THE DRESSING

2 tablespoon red-wine vinegar

1/4 cup Dijon mustard

Salt and freshly ground black pepper, to taste

2 tablespoons olive oil

1/3 cup mayonnaise, preferably homemade or high-quality store-bought

2 tablespoons minced fresh parsley

Celery root has a very tough peel and discolors easily, so work quickly. Use a sharp sturdy paring knife to cut away the peel. Rub the white flesh with a little of the lemon juice.

Cut the celery root into chunks that will fit into the tube of a food processor fitted with the shredding blade. (You can also shred the celery root with a mandoline.) Shred the celery root, then toss in a large bowl with the remaining lemon juice and salt and cover tightly.

Cut the apple into julienne with a sharp knife or mandoline.

Toss with the shredded celery root and cover.

Prepare the dressing: In a warm medium bowl, whisk the vinegar, mustard, salt, and pepper. Gradually whisk in the oil until emulsified. Whisk in the mayonnaise. Season with additional salt and pepper, if desired.

Fold the dressing into the celery-root mixture and taste for seasoning. Cover and refrigerate until well-chilled. (The salad will keep for several days if kept covered and refrigerated.) When ready to serve, sprinkle with the parsley.

Succotash and Lobster

...

2 (1¹/₄ pound) lobsters
8 ears fresh corn, husked, silk removed
2 cups small shelled fresh lima beans
8 tablespoons (1 stick) unsalted butter
1 cup heavy cream or half and half

1 pinch ground cloves
1 pinch cayenne pepper
Salt and freshly ground white pepper, to taste
2 tablespoons fresh chives, snipped into ¹/₂-inch strips

In a large covered kettle, bring 6 quarts salted water to a rolling boil over high heat. Add the lobsters, cover, and cook for 10 minutes. Drain and cool under cold running water. With poultry shears, cut away the claw and tail shells and carefully remove the meat. If the lobsters are female, reserve the grainy red coral and chop finely. Cover and refrigerate the lobster meat and coral.

With a sharp knife, cut the kernels off the cob, slicing from the top of the ear downward, but not too close to the cob. You should have about 4 cups. Using a small spoon, scrape the pulp from the cobs into a medium bowl. Add the kernels and reserve.

In a medium saucepan of lightly salted boiling water, blanch the lima beans until almost tender, 3 to 5 minutes. Cool under cold running water. Drain and reserve.

In a large heavy nonreactive saucepan, melt the butter over medium heat. Add the cream. When it begins to steam, add the corn and its pulp and cook for 10 minutes, stirring often until the liquid thickens slightly. Add the lima beans and cook another 2 minutes until the beans are just tender. Add the lobster meat and cook an additional 3 minutes until the meat is warmed through. Season with the cloves, cayenne, salt, and pepper. Fold in the chives.

Spoon the succotash and lobster in equal proportions into 4 warm soup plates and serve.

Summer Salad

· · ·

SERVES 4

1 bunch red radishes, trimmed, scrubbed, and thinly sliced
1 bunch scallions, trimmed and thinly sliced (include some of the green)
1 medium cucumber, peeled, halved lengthwise, seeded, and diced

2 tablespoons chopped fresh dill
2 cups plain yogurt
Kosher salt and freshly ground white pepper, to taste

Mix all the ingredients together in a medium bowl. Cover and refrigerate for 1 hour or until well-chilled.

Caprese Salad

...

SERVES 4

4 ripe tomatoes
12 ounces fresh buffalo or whole-milk mozzarella
Sea or kosher salt and fresh ground black pepper to taste

$^1/_4$ cup extra-virgin olive oil
Whole sprigs of bush basil or fresh basil leaves sliced into thin ribbons

Slice the tomatoes and mozzarella into $^1/_4$-inch slices and salt and pepper each slice.

To serve, alternate the tomato and cheese slices on a serving platter. Drizzle with olive oil and sprinkle with the basil. Serve immediately.

Papaya with Shrimp and Yogurt-Dill Dressing

...

SERVES 4

FOR THE SAUCE

1 cup plain yogurt

1/4 cup mayonnaise, preferably homemade or high-quality store-bought

1 tablespoon fresh lemon juice

2 tablespoons chopped fresh dill

1/8 teaspoon cayenne pepper

Sea or kosher salt, to taste

1 pound medium shrimp, cooked

1 ripe papaya, peeled, and sliced into about 16 (1-inch) strips, (reserve some of the seeds)

Prepare the sauce: Combine all the ingredients, cover, and chill.

Shell the shrimp, leaving the tails intact. Refrigerate.

Divide the sliced papaya among 4 serving plates. Place the shrimp over the papaya and drizzle with the yogurt sauce. Sprinkle with some of the reserved papaya seeds. Serve chilled.

Pistou: Mediterranean Vegetable Soup with Basil Sauce

...

SERVES 8

FOR THE BASIL SAUCE

2 cups basil leaves, packed

$^1/_2$ cup grated Parmesan cheese

$^1/_4$ cup chopped walnuts

2 tablespoons tomato paste

3 cloves garlic, crushed

5 tablespoons extra-virgin olive oil

Salt and freshly ground black pepper, to taste

FOR THE SOUP

$^3/_4$ cup dried cannellini (white kidney) beans or 1 cup canned cannellini beans, drained

$^1/_4$ cup extra-virgin olive oil

1 pound ripe tomatoes, peeled, seeded, and chopped, or 1 (16-ounce) can Italian-style plum tomatoes

$2^1/_2$ quarts chicken or vegetable stock, homemade or low-sodium canned

2 carrots, peeled and sliced thin on the bias

2 medium leeks, trimmed, washed, cut into 2-inch julienne, and rewashed

$^1/_4$ pound string beans, trimmed and cut into $1^1/_2$-inch lengths

2 small zucchini, cut into small cubes

$^1/_2$ cup vermicelli, broken into small pieces

1 cup tender celery leaves (from the inner ribs), chopped

$^1/_8$ teaspoon saffron threads

Prepare the basil sauce: In a food processor fitted with the metal blade, pulse the basil, Parmesan cheese, walnuts, tomato paste, and garlic until puréed. Add the 5 tablespoons of olive oil and pulse until smooth. Season with salt and pepper. Place in a container, cover, and refrigerate until ready to use. (If you float a $^1/_4$-inch layer of olive oil over the basil sauce and keep it covered and refrigerated, it will keep for up to 2 weeks.)

Wash and pick over the dried beans and drain. In a medium saucepan of boiling water, cook the beans for 5 minutes. Remove from the heat, cover, and allow the beans to cool in their liquid. Return the cooled beans to the heat, bring to a boil, then simmer for 1 hour or until tender. (If using canned beans, carefully rinse twice in cold water, and drain.)

In a large nonreactive soup kettle, heat the $^1/_4$ cup of olive oil over medium heat. Add the tomatoes and cook for 3 minutes, or until they release their juice.

Add the stock and bring to a simmer. Add the carrots and leeks and simmer for 10 minutes. Add the string beans and the cannellini beans and simmer for 3 minutes. Add the zucchini, vermicelli, celery leaves, and saffron and simmer for 5 minutes until the pasta is tender. Stir in 2 tablespoons of the basil sauce and taste for seasoning.

Ladle the soup into warm soup plates and serve with the remaining basil sauce on the side.

Black Bean Soup

2 cups (1 pound) dried black beans
1/4 cup vegetable or olive oil
1 medium onion, finely chopped
2 garlic cloves, chopped

1 large tomato, peeled, seeded, and chopped
1/2 cup chopped fresh parsley
1/4 teaspoon chopped fresh thyme leaves

This is the way I learned to cook black beans when traveling in Brazil—the beans turn out perfectly. Wash and pick over the beans. Place them in a large nonreactive soup kettle and add enough water (about 3 quarts) to cover by 5 inches. Bring to a boil and cook for 2 minutes. Remove kettle from the heat, cover, and set aside for 6 hours or overnight.

Return the beans to a simmer and cook, partially covered, for 1 hour until the beans are almost, but not quite, tender.

In a small nonreactive sauce pan, heat the oil over medium heat. Add the onion and garlic and sauté for 5 minutes until the onion is translucent. Add the tomato and cook for 4 minutes. Stir in the parsley and thyme. Fold the tomato mixture into the beans and season with salt and pepper. Continue simmering the beans for another 30 minutes until the beans are tender.

Drain the beans, reserving the cooking liquid. Purée in a food processor fitted with the metal blade, adding some of the liquid to make a smooth soup. Transfer to a clean soup pot and stir in more liquid if the soup is too thick. Taste for seasoning. Serve in warm soup plates. (The soup can also be served chilled.)

SERVING SUGGESTIONS: If serving hot, add a tablespoon of dry sherry to each portion; or float a thin lemon slice, a bit of chopped hard-boiled egg, and chopped chives or scallions on top. If serving cold, add a little cooked chopped shrimp or lobster, a thin slice of lime, and accompany with any New Orleans or Caribbean hot sauce.

Purée of Pea Soup with Mint

3 cups frozen peas

1 tablespoon chopped fresh mint leaves

3 cups (or more if desired) chicken or vegetable stock, homemade or low-sodium canned, heated

Salt and freshly ground white pepper, to taste

1 to 1 1/2 cups heavy cream, milk, or a combination of sour cream and milk

In a large saucepan of boiling lightly salted water, cook the peas for 1 minute. Drain.

Using a food processor fitted with the metal blade, purée the peas and mint with 1/2 cup of the broth. Season with salt and pepper, and gradually add another cup of broth. Scrape the mixture into a medium saucepan, stir in the remaining 1 1/2 cups broth, and bring to a simmer over medium-low heat.

If serving hot, scald the heavy cream or milk. Whisk into the pea purée and simmer another 5 minutes. (If using the sour cream-milk combination, heat just until hot—do not simmer.) Add more liquid if you want a lighter soup. Taste for seasoning and serve.

If serving cold, transfer the pea mixture to a large bowl, whisk in the remaining 1 cup of broth, and cool. Whisk in chilled cream or milk and refrigerate until cold.

Fish Soup with Rouille

FOR THE ROUILLE

1 small red bell pepper

1 (2-inch-thick) slice French bread

$1/4$ cup red-wine vinegar

2 egg yolks, at room temperature

4 garlic cloves, chopped

$1/4$ teaspoon crushed hot-pepper flakes

Salt and freshly ground black pepper, to taste

About 1 cup olive oil

2 tablespoons boiling water

FOR THE CROUTONS

1 loaf French bread, cut into $1/2$-inch-thick slices

FOR THE FISH STOCK

3 pounds fish bones, including heads, backbone,
    and tails (use the bones of any white fish; avoid
    oily fish such as mackerel, bluefish, and
    salmon)

2 medium onions, chopped

2 celery ribs, chopped

2 carrots, chopped

1 small fennel bulb, chopped

2 strips orange zest

2 sprigs fresh thyme, or 1 teaspoon dried

2 bay leaves

5 black peppercorns

6 fresh parsley sprigs

2 cups dry white wine

FOR THE SOUP

$1/4$ cup extra-virgin olive oil

1 medium onion, chopped

2 pounds ripe tomatoes, peeled, seeded, and
    chopped

2 quarts fresh fish stock

2 medium carrots, cut into 2-inch julienne

2 small leeks, washed, cut into 2-inch
    julienne, rewashed, and drained

1 small celery heart (white part only) cut into
    2-inch julienne

$1/4$ cup chopped flat-leaf parsley

$1/4$ cup chopped fresh basil

1 teaspoon chopped fresh thyme leaves

1 teaspoon chopped fresh tarragon leaves

$1/4$ teaspoon saffron threads, crumbled

2 ounces Ricard or Pernod (optional)

Salt and freshly ground black pepper, to taste

Grated Parmesan cheese, for serving

Prepare rouille: Using a long handled fork, char the pepper on all sides over a gas flame or charcoal grill. When the skin bubbles and blackens, remove from the heat. When cool enough to handle, scrape away the charred skin, remove the stem, and scrape away the seeds.

In a small bowl, let the bread slice soak up the vinegar, then squeeze out the vinegar.

In a food processor fitted with the metal blade, combine the roasted pepper, bread, egg yolks, garlic, hot-pepper flakes, salt, and pepper. Pulse the mixture on and off until smooth. With the machine running, gradually add the olive oil in a slow steady stream and process until the mixture is the consistency of thick mayonnaise. Add the boiling water to lighten the mixture. Scrape the mixture into a bowl, cover, and set aside. (The rouille can be prepared 1 day ahead and refrigerated. Bring to room temperature before use.)

Prepare the croutons: Preheat the oven to 350°F. Place the bread on a baking sheet and bake 10 to 15 minutes until golden brown. Set the croutons aside.

Prepare the stock: Rinse the fish bones well under cold running water, checking to be sure the gills have been removed.

Place the fish bones and all the remaining ingredients in a large soup kettle, and add enough cold water to cover. Bring the stock to a boil over high heat. Reduce the heat to low and simmer for 1 hour. Remove from the heat and cool.

Line a strainer or colander with a damp kitchen towel or a

double thickness of damp cheesecloth and place it over a clean pot. Ladle the stock into the strainer, then add the bones and vegetables. Let the stock drain for 15 minutes. Do not press out the juices. Set aside. (Makes about $2\frac{1}{2}$ quarts; the stock can be prepared up to 2 days ahead if kept covered and refrigerated, or frozen for up to 1 month.)

Prepare the soup: In a large nonreactive stock pot, heat the olive oil over medium heat. Add the onion and sauté until wilted and translucent, about 10 minutes. Add the tomatoes and their juice and simmer for 10 minutes. Add the stock, bring to a simmer, and cook for 5 minutes. Add the carrots, leeks, and celery and simmer for 10 minutes or until the vegetables are tender but not overcooked.

Stir in the parsley, basil, thyme, tarragon, saffron, and optional Ricard and simmer for another 10 minutes. Season with salt and pepper.

Ladle the soup into warm soup plates. Spread some of the rouille on top of a crouton and float on top of the soup. Accompany with grated Parmesan cheese and additional croutons and rouille.

Note: To substitute for fresh fish stock, bring 1 quart of chicken broth (preferably fresh, or use low-sodium canned), 1 quart water, 1 cup dry white wine, and 3 or 4 fish bouillon cubes to a simmer over high heat, then simmer for 10 minutes.

Main Courses

Red Scallop Pasta

5 tablespoons unsalted butter
1 cup fresh bread crumbs
1 pound spaghetti
4 tablespoons olive oil
2 garlic cloves, minced
2 cups fresh or canned plum tomatoes, peeled, seeded, and chopped

1 pint fresh bay scallops
1 teaspoon crushed hot-pepper flakes, or to taste
1/3 cup chopped fresh flat-leaf parsley
Salt and freshly ground black pepper, to taste

In a medium saucepan, melt 2 tablespoons of the butter over medium heat. Add the bread crumbs and cook, stirring occasionally, until toasted and golden, about 2 to 3 minutes. Pour crumbs out onto paper toweling and set aside.

In a large kettle of lightly salted boiling water, cook the spaghetti until al dente, about 12 minutes.

Meanwhile, in a large skillet over medium-low heat, melt the remaining 3 tablespoons butter with the oil. Add the garlic and sauté for 2 minutes until golden. Add the tomatoes and bring to a simmer, mashing down on them with a wooden spoon. When the sauce is heated through, add the scallops and cook for 3 minutes until the scallops are barely opaque. Stir in the pepper flakes and parsley and cook for another minute. Season with salt and pepper.

Drain the pasta. In a large skillet over high heat, add a few ladles of sauce. Add the pasta and another ladle of sauce and toss to coat. Divide the pasta into 4 warm bowls. Divide the remaining sauce among the bowls and sprinkle generously with the toasted bread crumbs. Serve immediately.

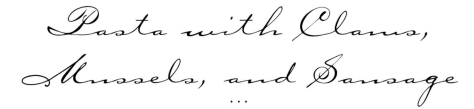

Pasta with Clams, Mussels, and Sausage

...

SERVES 4–5

12 baby artichokes, tough outer leaves discarded

$^1/_2$ lemon

$^1/_4$ cup olive oil, or as needed

2 garlic cloves, crushed

1 medium red bell pepper, cored, seeded, deveined, and julienned

3 shallots, peeled and chopped

3 ripe medium tomatoes, peeled, seeded, and chopped, or 2 cups canned Italian-style plum tomatoes

18 small littleneck clams, scrubbed

2 pounds mussels, scrubbed and debearded

$^3/_4$ pound spicy-hot pork sausage links, pricked with a fork

1 pound spaghetti or linguine

$^1/_2$ cup chopped fresh flat-leaf parsley

Keep a large kettle of lightly salted water at a near boil for the pasta.

Cut the artichokes in half lengthwise and rub them with the lemon. Using a small paring knife, scrape away the thistly chokes. In a large deep nonreactive saucepan, heat the olive oil over medium heat. Add the artichokes and garlic, cover, and sauté, shaking the pan occasionally, until the artichokes are tender, about 10 minutes. Using a slotted spoon, transfer the artichokes to a bowl and discard the garlic.

In the same saucepan, sauté the red pepper and shallots for 5 minutes until the peppers soften, adding a little more olive oil, if necessary. Add the tomatoes and bring to a simmer, mashing down on them with a wooden spoon. Return the artichokes to the pan, partially cover, and reduce the heat to low.

Place the cleaned clams and mussels in the freezer for 10 minutes while you prepare the sausages. In a medium skillet over medium heat, cook the sausages, turning occasionally until browned, about 10 minutes. When cool enough to handle, slice them into $^1/_2$-inch rounds, add to the sauce, and cover. Bring the kettle of water up to a full boil, add the pasta, and cook until al dente, about 12 minutes.

While pasta is cooking, raise the heat under the sauce to medium-high and cover for 2 minutes to create a head of steam. Add the clams and mussels to the sauce and cover. Cook, shaking the pan occasionally, until the clams and mussels open, about 4 minutes. Turn off the heat and set aside with the saucepan lid ajar.

Drain the pasta and return to the kettle. Add a ladle or two of the sauce and heat briefly. Divide the pasta among warm serving bowls and top with more sauce and the shellfish.

Lemon Risotto

...

5 cups chicken stock, homemade or low-sodium canned
5 tablespoons unsalted butter
1 tablespoon olive oil
1 small onion, finely chopped
1 1/2 cups arborio rice

3/4 cup good-quality vodka
3/4 cup fresh lemon juice
Zest of 1 1/2 lemons, finely minced
1 cup grated Parmesan cheese
Salt and freshly ground white pepper, to taste

In a medium saucepan, bring the broth to a simmer over medium heat. Reduce the heat to low and keep the broth at a bare simmer.

In a large, heavy saucepan, heat the butter and oil over medium heat. When the butter has melted, add the onions and sauté until translucent, about 6 to 8 minutes. Add the rice and coat with the mixture stirring constantly with a wooden spoon.

Add the vodka, stirring constantly until the rice absorbs the liquid, about 3 minutes. Add the lemon juice and continue stirring until the liquid is absorbed. Add the broth, a ladle at a time, stirring constantly. Continue adding until you reach a point where the liquid is absorbed and the rice is creamy and al dente, about 25 minutes.

Fold in the lemon zest and 1/2 cup of the Parmesan cheese. Season with salt and pepper.

Serve immediately, accompanied by the remaining 1/2 cup of Parmesan cheese.

Note: Classic risotto is prepared using only broth for the cooking liquid. Two of my favorite variations on the traditional risotto are adding steamed asparagus tips and cooked fresh peas when the rice is al dente; or substituting the first ladle of stock with 1 cup of good Italian red wine and adding sautéed porcini mushrooms just when the rice is al dente.

Stewed Apples
with Macaroni and Cheese

···

SERVES 4–5

FOR THE APPLES

4 firm Golden Delicious apples, peeled, halved, cored,
   and sliced $1/2$-inch thick
$1/2$ teaspoon grated lemon zest
1 tablespoon granulated sugar (optional)

FOR THE MACARONI

7 tablespoons unsalted butter
1 tablespoon vegetable oil
4 medium onions, thinly sliced
1 pound small elbow macaroni
10 ounces Gruyère cheese, shredded
Salt and freshly ground pepper, to taste
4 tablespoons chopped fresh chives

In a medium nonreactive saucepan, toss the apples with the lemon zest, adding the sugar if you like slightly sweeter apples. Cover and cook over medium heat for 10 minutes, or until the apples give up some of their juice, but keep their shape. Shake the pan from time to time to prevent sticking. Set aside.

In a large skillet, melt 4 tablespoons of the butter and heat the oil over medium-high heat. Add the onions and sauté until crisp and golden brown, about 10 minutes. While the onions are cooking, cook the macaroni in a large kettle of lightly salted boiling water until just tender, about 10 to 12 minutes.

Drain the macaroni. Add the remaining butter, the cheese, salt, and pepper and toss all together until the cheese melts. Spoon into 4 warm soup plates and top with onions. Sprinkle with the chives and serve with the stewed apples on the side.

Chicken Pot Pie

...

SERVES 4

1 (3 1/2 to 4-pound) chicken, wings removed, washed, and dried

1 medium tomato, blanched and peeled

2 cups chicken stock, homemade or low-sodium canned

3 small carrots, cut into 2-inch julienne

2 small turnips, peeled and quartered

8 small white onions, blanched and peeled

1/4 pound small string beans, trimmed

1/3 cup fresh or frozen peas

6 tablespoons unsalted cold butter, cut into chunks

1 small black truffle, thinly sliced and julienned (optional)

Sea salt and freshly ground black pepper, to taste

1/2 pound homemade puff pastry, or 1 defrosted frozen puff pastry sheet

1 egg, beaten

Preheat the oven to 450°F.

Place the chicken in a round 3-quart ovenproof tureen.

Core the tomato, cut into eighths, and remove the seeds.

In a medium saucepan, bring the broth to a boil and reduce to a simmer. Add the carrots, turnips, onions, string beans, and peas and cook for 3 minutes. Strain, reserving the broth. Cool the vegetables under cold running water, and drain. Add the vegetables and tomato (and frozen peas, if using) to the tureen. Dot with butter and sprinkle with the optional truffle. Season with salt and pepper.

Roll out the puff pastry on a lightly floured cold surface, to about a 3/16-inch thickness. Cut out a circle of pastry about 2 inches larger than the diameter of the tureen. Brush the circle lightly with the beaten egg. Fit it over the tureen, brushed-side-down, pressing the overhanging pastry against the sides of the tureen. Brush the top side lightly with additional egg. Bake for 10 minutes. Carefully cover the pastry loosely with heavy aluminum foil and continue baking for 35 minutes until puffed and golden brown. Turn the oven off. Leave the tureen in the closed oven for 20 minutes, then remove.

Bring the tureen to the table and carefully cut off the crust, just inside the rim. Set the crust aside. Remove the bird and carve it on a separate platter. Serve in warm soup plates with the vegetables, juices, and a bit of the crust.

Roast Chicken

...

SERVES 4

1 (4-pound) chicken, neck, giblets, and wing tips reserved
Kosher salt and freshly ground black pepper, to taste
1 bunch tarragon sprigs (about 1 cup)
1 large lemon

2 tablespoons rendered goose fat or olive oil
1 medium onion, halved
1 cup chicken stock, homemade or low-sodium canned, or substitute water
  if necessary

Preheat the oven to 425°F.
Discard the fat from the cavity of the chicken. Wash the chicken and pat it dry. Salt and pepper the cavity. Tuck a few small sprigs of tarragon between the skin and breast meat. Place the remainder inside the cavity. Prick the entire surface of the lemon with a fork and place the lemon inside of the cavity.

Truss the chicken and rub the skin with the goose fat. Season the exterior of the chicken with salt and pepper. Place it on its side on the rack of a roasting pan. Scatter the neck, wingtips, and onion halves alongside the chicken. Set aside the liver. (Freeze the remaining giblets for future use, such as making stock.)

Place the chicken on the center rack of the oven and roast for 20 minutes. Baste, then turn it on its other side, and roast for another 20 minutes. Baste again, turn the chicken breast-side-up, and roast for 20 minutes longer.

Reduce the oven temperature to 375°F. and baste again. Continue roasting until the juices run clear when thigh joint is pierced with a sharp paring knife, about 15 more minutes. During the last 10 minutes or so, salt and pepper the liver and add to the chicken juices in the pan. Turning only once, roast the liver for about 8 minutes, depending on its size.

Transfer the chicken and liver to a warm platter. Turn the oven off and place the chicken in the oven with the door ajar for 10 minutes or longer while you make the sauce.

Spoon off the excess fat from the roasting pan and place the pan on the stove over high heat. Add the broth and bring to a boil. Deglaze by scraping up the browned bits in the pan with a wooden spoon. Reduce the heat and simmer for 5 minutes or until the sauce begins to thicken. Strain the sauce through a fine sieve and pour into a warm sauceboat. Serve with the chicken and liver.

Osso Buco

6 veal hind shanks, sawed by the butcher into 2-inch-thick pieces
1 veal foreshank, sawed into 2-inch-thick pieces, optional (see Note)
Salt and freshly ground black pepper, to taste
1 cup all-purpose flour
3 tablespoons unsalted butter
3 tablespoons olive oil
1 cup finely chopped onions
1 cup finely chopped carrots
1 cup finely chopped celery
1 cup dry white wine
1 cup (about 1 pound) ripe tomatoes, peeled, seeded, and chopped, or canned

Italian-style tomatoes, chopped
2 cups chicken stock, homemade or low-sodium canned
2 garlic cloves, crushed
2 bay leaves
3 sprigs parsley

FOR THE GREMOLATA
1 tablespoon minced orange zest
1 tablespoon minced lemon zest
2 garlic cloves, minced
1/2 cup chopped fresh parsley

Preheat oven to 325° F. Tie the veal shanks vertically with kitchen string so the meat will not fall away from the bone during cooking time. (No need to tie the foreshank pieces, if using.) Season with salt and pepper, then toss liberally with the flour, and dust off the excess.

In a large sauté pan, melt the butter and heat the oil over medium heat. In uncrowded batches, brown the shanks on both sides for about 8 to 10 minutes. Transfer to a large ovenproof casserole.

Add the onions, carrots, and celery to the sauté pan and sauté for about 10 minutes, allowing them to brown slightly. Transfer the vegetables to the casserole. Deglaze the pan with the wine, scraping up the browned bits that have adhered to the pan.

Add the tomatoes and broth and bring to a simmer. Pour into the casserole and add the garlic, bay leaves, and parsley. Cover and bake for 1 1/2 hours, or when the shanks are fork tender.

Prepare the gremolata: In a small bowl, combine all the ingredients, cover, and set aside. Remove the shanks from the casserole. Degrease the cooking liquid and season with salt and pepper. Stir in 1 tablespoon of the gremolata.

Cut away the string from the shanks and divide the meat among 6 warm dinner plates. Spoon on some of the sauce and sprinkle with the remaining gremolata.

Note: For a richer and more gelatinous sauce, brown the optional foreshank along with the hind shanks and cook in the sauce. There won't be much meat, but it will still be delicious.

Braised Lamb Shanks with White Beans

...

SERVES 6

6 meaty lamb shanks (about 1 pound each)

Salt and freshly ground black pepper, to taste

$1/4$ cup olive oil

2 medium onions, chopped

2 cups robust red wine

2 ripe tomatoes (about $1^1/2$ cups), peeled, seeded, and chopped, or use drained, canned Italian-style tomatoes

2 garlic cloves, crushed

1 sprig fresh rosemary, or $1/2$ teaspoon dried

1 sprig fresh thyme, or $1/4$ teaspoon dried

1 (2-inch) strip orange zest

3 cups chicken stock, approximately, homemade or low-sodium canned

4 cups cooked white beans or canned cannellini beans, carefully rinsed and drained

$1/2$ cup chopped parsley

Liberally season the shanks with salt and pepper. In a large skillet, heat the oil over medium heat. In uncrowded batches, brown the shanks on all sides, about 10 minutes. Transfer the shanks to a large ovenproof casserole. Add the onions to the skillet and sauté for 10 minutes until lightly browned and limp. Scrape into the casserole. Deglaze the pan with the wine, scraping up the browned bits that have adhered to the skillet. Pour into the casserole. Add the tomatoes, garlic, rosemary, thyme, and orange zest, with enough stock to barely cover the shanks. Cover and bake at 350° for $1^1/2$ hours or until the meat is fork-tender but still clings to the bone.

Remove the casserole from the oven. Transfer the shanks to a platter and cover to keep warm. Degrease the cooking liquid and season with salt and pepper. Add the beans and parsley and bury the shanks in the beans and sauce.

Cover and return to the oven to bake until the beans absorb some of the sauce, about 15 minutes.

Lamb Stew

8 tablespoons unsalted butter

3 tablespoons vegetable oil

3 pounds boneless lamb shoulder, cut into 2-inch pieces

2 pounds lamb breast with bone, sawed by the butcher into 2-inch pieces

Salt and freshly ground black pepper, to taste

4 cups lamb or chicken stock, homemade or low-sodium
  canned

1/4 cup scotch (optional)

1/2 teaspoon crushed dried sage

1/2 teaspoon dried thyme

4 medium russet potatoes, peeled and quartered lengthwise

About 20 baby carrots, peeled

About 20 small white boiling onions

4 small turnips

2 tablespoons sugar

1/2 cup chopped fresh parsley

Preheat oven to 275° F.
In a large skillet melt 2 tablespoons of the butter with 1 tablespoon of the oil over high heat. Season one-third of the lamb with the salt and pepper. Brown the lamb on all sides until lightly crusted, about 10 minutes. Transfer to a large casserole or Dutch oven and set aside. Pour off the fat from the skillet. Add 1 cup of stock and bring to a boil, scraping up the browned bits that adhere to the pan. Pour into the casserole with the lamb. Repeat with the remaining lamb, using 2 tablespoons butter and 1 tablespoon oil for browning each batch and deglazing with 1 cup broth.

Add the remaining 1 cup stock with the optional scotch, sage, and thyme. Cover and bake for 1½ hours. Remove from the heat, uncover, and cool to room temperature. When cool, cover and refrigerate for 24 hours.

Preheat the oven to 300° F. and remove the casserole from the refrigerator. Skim off the film of cold fat on the surface. Cover the casserole and bake for 30 minutes while you prepare the vegetables.

In a pot of lightly salted boiling water, cook the potatoes for 10 minutes until slightly resistant when pierced with a knife. Transfer the potatoes with a slotted spoon to a bowl and set aside. Add the carrots to the boiling water and cook for 4 minutes until slightly resistant when pierced with a knife. Drain and set aside. When the stew has baked for 30 minutes, add the partially cooked potatoes and carrots and bake for an additional 30 minutes.

Meanwhile, trim the onions and cut an "X" into the root end of each. Bring a pan of lightly salted water to a boil. Add the onions and cook until tender, about 8 minutes. Drain and rinse them under cold running water. Drain again and remove the outer skins. Set aside.

Peel the turnips and halve into ¼-inch wedges. Bring a saucepan of lightly salted water to a boil. Add the turnip wedges and cook until crisp-tender, about 4 minutes. Drain and rinse under cold running water. Drain again and set aside.

In a medium sauté pan, melt the remaining 2 tablespoons of butter over medium heat and add the onions and turnips. Sprinkle with the sugar and continue to cook, tossing often, until the onions and turnips are golden and caramelized, about 10 to 15 minutes.

To serve, ladle the stewed lamb, potatoes, carrots, and some of the sauce onto warm plates or soup plates. Divide the onions and turnips among the plates and sprinkle with the parsley.

Steak Salad with Vegetables

...

SERVES 4

FOR THE VINAIGRETTE

1 medium morel, cleaned and chppped (about ¹/4 cup)

1 cup imported peanut oil

¹/4 cup red-wine vinegar

1 teaspoon Dijon mustard

Salt and freshly ground pepper, to taste

FOR THE SALAD

2 heads bibb lettuce, trimmed, washed, and thoroughly dried

1 small head red Boston lettuce, trimmed, washed and thoroughly dried

1 cup hulled green peas (about ³/4 pound)

Juice of ¹/2 lemon

1 cup shelled fava beans (about 1 pound)

1 bunch scallions, cut 2 inches long and trimmed (include some of the green)

16 tiny new potatoes, washed

1 cup chicken stock

5 to 7 ounces fresh small morels, cleaned and trimmed just before cooking

FOR THE TOMATO RELISH

3 ripe tomatoes (about 1 pound), blanched, peeled, seeded, with juice removed and reserved

1 cumin seed, peeled and finely crushed

1 tablespoon extra-virgin olive oil

Salt and freshly ground pepper to taste

FOR THE STEAK

1 2 to 2 ¹/2-pound boneless sirloin (with fat), at room temperature

Kosher salt and freshly ground black pepper, to taste

1 cup chervil sprigs, stems removed and very loosely packed

In a small pan, combine the chopped morels with oil and heat over low heat until oil is warm to the touch. Set aside to steep for two hours, then remove and discard morel pieces. In a bowl, combine the vinegar, mustard, salt, and pepper, and mix thoroughly. Gradually whisk in ³/4 cup of the morel oil, or more, depending on acidity of the vinegar. Set aside.

For the salad: tear the lettuce into bite-size pieces, wrap in paper toweling, and refrigerate. In a small pot of lightly salted boiling water, add the peas and a little of the lemon juice and cook the peas for 6 to 10 minutes, until tender. Drain under cold running water and drain again. Set aside.

Repeat the same process for the fava beans, adding the remaining lemon juice and setting aside; the scallions, simmering them for 1 to 2 minutes, draining them thoroughly and setting them aside on paper toweling; and the potatoes, cooking them for about 12 minutes, or until tender, draining thoroughly, and setting them aside in a covered pot. (If the potatoes are larger than the size of a quarter, halve or quarter them.)

In a small saucepan, heat the stock over medium heat. Add the small morels and simmer for 5 to 7 minutes, or until tender. Drain and reserve, saving the stock for some other use.

Prepare the relish: chop the tomatoes very fine or pulse once or twice in a food processor. Add the cumin, oil, salt, and pepper. If too thick, add a little of the reserved juice of the tomato and chill. Preheat the oven to 325°F. In a large skillet, heat about one tablespoon of the remaining oil. Season the steak with kosher salt and pepper and raise the heat. Sear the steak for about 5 minutes on each side, until lightly crusted and browned. Transfer steak to the oven and bake for 8 to 12 minutes, or to liking. Let meat rest while you cut the greens.

In a large bowl, toss the lettuce with enough vinaigrette to coat, then divide among four plates. Repeat the process with the vegetables and morels. Trim the fat from the steak and slice the meat into thin strips. Arrange the slices over the greens and vegetables in a lattice fashion and sprinkle with chervil. Add a little relish to the side of each plate and serve.

Meatloaf

1 pound lean ground beef

1/2 pound lean ground veal

1/2 pound lean ground pork

1 medium onion, finely chopped

1 garlic clove, minced

1 teaspoon chopped fresh tarragon leaves or 1/2 teaspoon dried

1/4 cup chopped fresh parsley

1 cup (about 4 thin slices) fresh whole-wheat bread crumbs

1 egg

1/2 cup bottled chili sauce

1 tablespoon heavy cream

Salt and freshly ground black pepper, to taste

4 thick slices slab smoked bacon, cut 1/4-inch thick

3/4 cup sour cream, at room temperature

Hot Hot Tomato Chutney (page 89)

Preheat the oven to 325°F.

In a large mixing bowl, combine all of the ingredients except the bacon, sour cream, and chutney. Mix well.

Shape the mixture to fit into a 9 x 5-inch loaf pan. Cover the top with the bacon slices, tucking the bacon between the meat loaf and sides of the pan.

Cover with foil and bake for 1 hour. Remove the foil and bake for an additional 15 minutes. Remove and discard the bacon. Using a bulb baster, suction off and reserve the cooking liquid. Let stand, then skim off the fat from the top.

Measure 1/4 cup of the cooking liquid and stir into the reserved sour cream. Blend thoroughly and serve with the meat loaf, accompanied by the chutney.

Choucroute

2 pounds fresh or packaged (not canned) sauerkraut

3 tablespoons goose fat or unsalted butter

2 large onions, chopped

2 garlic cloves, minced

3 cups chicken stock, homemade or low-sodium canned

1 1/3 cups dry white wine

1 ounce high-quality aromatic gin, such as Bombay, or 1 teaspoon juniper berries, slightly crushed

1 tart green apple, peeled, cored, and chopped

1/2 teaspoon caraway seeds

1/4 teaspoon dried thyme

Salt and freshly ground black pepper, to taste

2 pounds French garlic sausage, pricked

1 pound slab bacon with rind, in 1 piece

4 bratwursts, pricked

4 weisswursts, pricked

8 smoked pork chops

1/4 cup chopped fresh parsley

Place the sauerkraut in a large bowl and cover with cold water. Let stand for 20 minutes. Drain, wash, and taste. If still too briny, repeat once or twice more as necessary and drain well, squeezing out the sauerkraut a handful at a time. Fluff the sauerkraut strands and reserve.

Preheat the oven to 325°F. In a heavy 5-quart nonreactive pot, melt the goose fat over medium heat. Add the onions and garlic and sauté for 10 minutes until the onions are translucent. Add the stock, 1 cup of the wine, gin, and apple. Bring to a simmer. Add the sauerkraut and stir in the caraway, thyme, salt, and pepper. Cover and simmer, stirring occasionally to prevent sticking, about 30 minutes.

While the sauerkraut is cooking, place the sausage in a saucepan and cover with cold water. Bring to a boil, then reduce the heat and simmer until heated through, about 10 to 15 min-utes, depending on their size, Remove and set aside in the water.

Place the smoked bacon in a shallow saucepan, cover with cold water, and bring to a boil. Reduce the heat and simmer for 10 minutes to reduce the smoke and salt flavors. Drain. When cool enough to handle, slice the bacon away from the rind and cut into 1/4-inch-thick slices.

Transfer half of the sauerkraut mixture to a large oven-proof casserole. Add the sausages, wursts, and smoked pork chops and cover with the remaining sauerkraut. Bury some of the bacon slices into the sauerkraut and place the remainder on top. Pour in the remaining wine and bake for 1 hour until most of the liquid has evaporated.

Sprinkle with the parsley. Serve directly from the casserole or make an arrangement on a large platter. Serve with parsleyed boiled potatoes, rye bread, and a variety of mustards.

Shepherd's Pie

...

SERVES 5–6

2 cups lamb stock or chicken stock, homemade or low-sodium canned,
   including any remaining leftover lamb roast juices
5 tablespoons unsalted butter
1 medium onion, finely chopped
1 tablespoon red-wine vinegar
1 teaspoon tomato paste
3 cups leftover cooked leg of lamb, trimmed of all fat and gristle and cut
   into 1-inch cubes

1 tablespoon Worcestershire sauce
1/8 teaspoon cayenne pepper, to taste
Salt and freshly ground pepper, to taste
1/4 cup finely chopped fresh parsley or dill
2 tablespoons grated Parmesan cheese
3 cups mashed potatoes (see Note)

In a small saucepan, add the stock and leftover lamb juices and simmer over medium heat until reduced by half, about 15 minutes. Set aside.

In a large skillet, melt 4 tablespoons of the butter over medium heat. Add the onion and cook for 6 minutes until wilted. Add the reduced stock and bring to a simmer. Stir in the vinegar and tomato paste and simmer for 1 minute. Add the cubed lamb, Worcestershire sauce, and cayenne pepper. Season with salt and pepper and cook for another 2 minutes until the meat absorbs some of the sauce. Stir in the parsley and remove from the heat.

Butter a 3-quart souffle dish or deep baking dish with the remaining 1 tablespoon of butter. Spread a thin layer of mashed potatoes on the bottom of the dish, about 1 cup. Add the lamb mixture and spread the remaining potato mixture over the top (or place the potato mixture in a pastry bag fitted with a large star tube and pipe the potatoes on top.) Lightly dust the potatoes with the Parmesan cheese.

Bake for 30 minutes until the potatoes are lightly browned and the lamb mixture is bubbling. Serve with the Plum Ketchup (page 95).

Note: Make 3 cups of mashed potatoes following the instructions for Herbed Mashed Potatoes with Roquefort Cheese (page 81), but eliminate the herbs and cheese. Use as much of the milk mixture to make a smooth purée. The mashed potatoes should be smooth but still hold their shape. (If using leftover mashed potatoes, bring them to room temperature and mix in one whole egg.)

Marinated Grilled Salmon

...

SERVES 6

FOR THE MARINADE

6 tablespoons soy sauce

2 tablespoons raw cane sugar or light brown sugar

1 teaspoon wasabi mustard, or to taste

Sea salt and freshly ground pepper, to taste

$1/2$ cup Canadian or rye whisky

2 teaspoons peeled and grated fresh ginger

2 garlic cloves, minced

$1/2$ cup canola oil, plus extra for brushing the grill

6 (8-ounce) center-cut salmon fillets, about $1^1/2$-inches thick, skin intact

Prepare the marinade: In a medium bowl combine the soy sauce with the sugar, wasabi, salt, and pepper. Add the whisky, ginger, and garlic. Gradually whisk in the oil. Place in a container, cover, and refrigerate overnight.

Using tweezers, pull away any bones from the salmon fillets. Place them, skin-side-down, in a large shallow pan. Shake the marinade well and pour over the fillets. Cover and refrigerate for 4 to 6 hours.

Build a charcoal fire in an outdoor grill. When the coals are ash-covered and glowing, use a brush or paper toweling to oil the grill, being careful not to use so much that it will drip onto the coals and cause them to flare up. (Place a sheet of punctured foil on top of the coals to avoid this problem.)

Place the fish fillets on the grill, skin-side-down and brush them with the marinade. Cook the fish for 5 minutes, brushing twice with the marinade. Gently slide a metal spatula between the skin and the flesh, press down on the skin and the grill, and pry up the flesh, separating it from the skin that will adhere to the grill. Turn the flesh over, placing on the adhered skin on the grill. Continue cooking and basting another 3 to 4 minutes until the flesh is opaque but the center is still slightly rare. Transfer to a warm platter (leave the skin on the grill) and serve immediately.

Grilled Swordfish with Salt Crust and Gin-Lime Butter

SERVES 6–8

FOR THE FISH
1 (4 pound) piece of swordfish, about 2-inches thick
1/4 pound unsalted butter, melted
1/2 cup fine sea salt

FOR THE GIN-LIME BUTTER
1/4 cup dry gin
3 tablespoon fresh lime juice
1/4 pound plus 4 tablespoons (1 1/4 stick) cold unsalted butter,
   cut into bits, chilled

Prepare the fish: Pat the swordfish dry with paper toweling and place on a large platter or pan.

Brush the top side with half of the melted butter. Dredge liberally with half of the salt.

Refrigerate for 20 minutes until the butter has congealed. Carefully turn the fish, brush the other side with the remaining melted butter and dredge with the remaining salt. Refrigerate for another 20 minutes, or until ready to grill. Build a charcoal fire in an outdoor grill.

Prepare the gin-lime butter: In a small nonreactive saucepan carefully bring the gin and lime juice to a simmer over medium heat. Be sure not to splash any of the liquid into the burner or the gin could ignite. Cook until reduced to a thick glaze, about 7 minutes.

Remove from the heat and whisk in 2 tablespoons of the butter, piece by piece. Return to low heat and, whisking constantly, add the remaining butter piece by piece. The sauce should have the texture and consistency of a thick creamy hollandaise. Remove from the heat. Set aside and keep warm until ready to serve with the fish.

When the coals are dusty and glowing, spread them out in the grill, banking them slightly against the sides. Place a sheet of heavy foil in the center. (This will prevent the melting butter from dripping onto the coals, flaring up, and burning the fish.)

Grill the fish for 10 minutes. Turn and cook for 7 more minutes. If the butter should flame up, cover the grill for a minute or two until the flames die down. The fish should be moist and tender. Cut the fish crosswise into thick slices and serve with the gin-lime butter.

Moqueca:
Bahia Fish Stew

...

2 pounds fish steaks, such as halibut, monkfish, tilefish, or swordfish

Salt and freshly ground white pepper, to taste

3 tablespoons fresh lime juice

3 tablespoons olive oil

2 medium onions, chopped

1 medium red bell pepper, cored, seeded, deveined, and chopped

1 medium green bell pepper, cored, seeded, deveined, and chopped

1 garlic clove crushed

3 large ripe tomatoes, peeled, seeded, and chopped

1 pound hubbard squash or pumpkin, peeled and cut into $1/2$-inch cubes

1 cup fresh or canned unsweetened coconut milk

1 tablespoon good-quality dende oil (see Note)

2 green plantains, peeled and sliced into 1-inch-thick rounds

$1/2$ cup chopped fresh cilantro

4 scallions, chopped (include some of the green)

Boiled rice and hot pepper sauce, for serving

Season the fish with salt and pepper and drizzle with 2 tablespoons of the lime juice. Set aside.

In an ovenproof casserole, heat the olive oil over medium heat. Add the onions and sauté until wilted, about 5 minutes. Add the red and green peppers and garlic and sauté until wilted, about 8 minutes. Add the tomatoes and squash and bring to a simmer. Stir in the coconut milk and dende oil and bring to a simmer. Add the plantains and cilantro, season with salt and pepper, and bury the fish in the sauce. Bake for 20 minutes until the fish flakes easily. Stir in the remaining 1 tablespoon lime juice and sprinkle with the scallions. Serve with rice and hot pepper sauce.

Note: Dende oil is a rich, orange-colored, palm oil and is used as a flavoring. It is high in cholesterol so use sparingly. You can find it at Brazilian and Latin American food stores.

Pumpkin Baked with Creamed Shrimp, Rio Style

SERVES 10–12

FOR THE PUMPKIN
1 medium (5 to 6-pound) pumpkin
Salt and freshly ground white pepper, to taste
1 large pinch ground mace
1 to 2 tablespoons vegetable oil, as needed

FOR THE FILLING
4 pounds medium shrimp, shelled and cleaned
1/4 cup (4 tablespoons) olive oil

3 large onions, peeled and finely chopped
1 pound tomatoes, peeled, seeded, and chopped
1 pound mascarpone cheese, at room temperature
4 ounces cream cheese (preferably Philadelphia brand), at room temperature
1 tablespoon chopped fresh cilantro
1/2 teaspoon chopped fresh oregano or 1/4 teaspoon dried
1/3 cup grated Parmesan cheese
Boiled white rice, for serving

Prepare the pumpkin: Preheat the oven to 375°F. Cut a circle about 3 inches down from the stem of the pumpkin to form a lid. Scoop out the seeds and clean away the fibers. Lightly salt and pepper the inside of the pumpkin and add the mace. Replace the lid to fit. Lightly rub the exterior of the pumpkin with vegetable oil and place on a well-oiled baking pan. Bake for 40 minutes, or until the interior flesh is almost tender and the exterior still firm. Do not overcook. Check by pressing your finger near the base of the pumpkin.

Remove the pumpkin from the oven and discard the lid. Using a bulb baster, extract and discard the liquid from inside the pumpkin. Cover the pumpkin shell with foil.

Prepare the filling: In a large bowl, toss the shrimp with 2 tablespoons of the olive oil and season with salt and pepper. Set aside.

In a large deep saucepan, heat the remaining 2 tablespoons oil over medium heat. Add the onions and sauté until translucent, about 5 minutes.

In a medium saucepan, cook the tomatoes over medium heat until the liquid evaporates, about 10 minutes.

Add the shrimp to the onion mixture and cook until the shrimp turn pink, about 3 minutes. Stir in the tomato mixture and cook for another minute. Add the mascarpone and cream cheese and stir until melted. Add the cilantro and taste for seasoning.

Raise the oven temperature to 500°F. The oven must be very hot. Check the well of the pumpkin again and remove any juice that may have collected. Pour the shrimp mixture into the pumpkin. Mix the oregano with the Parmesan cheese and sprinkle over the shrimp mixture.

Bake 10 to 12 minutes, or until the mixture bubbles lightly and the gratin is browned. Slide a wide spatula under the pumpkin, loosen gently, and carefully transfer to a warm serving platter.

To serve, scoop out some of the pumpkin meat with the shrimp mixture and accompany with boiled white rice.

Crab and Salmon Cakes

...

SERVES 4

FOR THE CAKES
8 ounces cooked salmon

8 ounces canned lump crabmeat, picked clean

3 scallions, minced (include some of the green)

$1/4$ cup cracker meal

$1/4$ cup mayonnaise, homemade or high-quality store-bought

1 egg, beaten

1 tablespoon finely chopped fresh parsley

1 teaspoon Dijon mustard

$1/8$ teaspoon grated nutmeg

$1/4$ teaspoon Old Bay Seasoning or $1/8$ teaspoon cayenne pepper

1 egg, beaten with 1 tablespoon water

1 cup fine bread crumbs, for dredging

FOR THE SAUCE
$1/2$ cup mayonnaise, homemade or high-quality store-bought

$1/2$ cup plain yogurt

1 tablespoon Dijon mustard

1 tablespoon catsup

1 tablespoon capers drained, dried, and chopped

1 tablespoon finely chopped sour pickles

1 tablespoon chopped fresh parsley

1 hard boiled egg, chopped (optional)

$1/4$ cup vegetable oil, for frying

Prepare the cakes: Remove any bones or skin from the salmon. In a medium bowl, flake the salmon with a fork. Add the crabmeat, scallions, cracker meal, mayonnaise, beaten egg, parsley, mustard, nutmeg, and Old Bay Seasoning. Mix well, cover, and refrigerate for 1 hour.

Shape the cold mixture into 8 small round cakes. Dip the cakes in the beaten-egg mixture and coat evenly with the breadcrumbs. Place the cakes on a large plate. Cover and refrigerate for 1 hour or more.

Prepare the sauce: In a small bowl, whisk the mayonnaise, yogurt, and mustard until smooth. Add the remaining ingredients, cover, and chill.

In a large skillet, heat the oil over medium heat until hot, but not smoking. Add the cakes and fry until golden on both sides, about 5 minutes. Drain on paper toweling. Serve over tossed salad and accompany with the sauce.

Serving suggestions: Use any type of mixed salad greens with diced fruit (such as peaches, mangos, or papayas), lightly dressed with vinaigrette; or substitute fresh corn kernels and black beans for the fruit.

Bourride with Aïoli

SERVES 4

FOR THE AÏOLI
2 tablespoons dried bread crumbs
2 tablespoons white-wine vinegar
4 egg yolks
12 garlic cloves, chopped
Salt and freshly ground white pepper, to taste
2 cups olive oil
1 tablespoon fresh lemon juice

FOR THE VEGETABLES
2 fennel bulbs, halved, cored, and each half cut lengthwise into thirds
3 cups chicken stock, homemade or low-sodium canned, or as needed
1 tablespoon unsalted butter

12 to 18 new potatoes, unpeeled and scrubbed
6 to 8 baby artichokes, tough outer leaves discarded
1/2 lemon
3 tablespoons olive oil

FOR THE BOURRIDE
2 quarts fish stock (see page 36)
2 pounds skinless fish fillets, such as snapper, striped bass, or monk fish, cut into 2-inch chunks
1/2 cup chopped fresh parsley

Toasted Croutons (see page 36)

Prepare the aïoli: Mix the bread crumbs with the vinegar. When absorbed, wring out the excess liquid in paper toweling.

Using the metal blade of a food processor, combine the bread crumb mixture, egg yolks, garlic, salt, and pepper. Pulse on and off until smooth. With the machine running, gradually add the olive oil in a slow steady stream and process until the aïoli is very thick. Add the lemon juice and 1 tablespoon of boiling water to lighten the mixture.

Using a rubber spatula, scrape the mixture into a bowl, cover, and refrigerate until ready to use. (The aïoli may be prepared 1 day ahead.)

Prepare the vegetables: Place the fennel wedges in a large sauté pan and add enough chicken stock to barely cover. Fit the pan with a buttered round of waxed paper. Bring the liquid to a simmer over medium heat. Cook the fennel for 20 minutes until fork tender. Set the fennel aside in the cooking liquid to keep warm.

Boil the potatoes in a large saucepan of lightly salted water until tender, about 15 minutes. Drain well. Wrap the potatoes in a clean kitchen towel, return to the pot, and cover to keep warm.

Cut the artichokes half lengthwise and rub them with the lemon. Using a small paring knife, scrape away the thistley chokes. In a nonreactive pan, heat the oil over medium heat, add the artichokes, cover and, shaking the pan occasionally, sauté until tender, about 10 minutes. Season with salt and pepper. Cover to keep warm and set aside.

Prepare the bourride: In a soup kettle, add the fish stock and bring to a simmer over medium heat. Rinse the fillets in cold water, drain, and pat dry. Add to the stock and simmer for 2 to 3 minutes until the fish is barely opaque. Place half of the aïoli in a medium bowl and gradually whisk in a ladle or two of the fish stock. Stir the aïoli-stock back into the kettle and cook another minute until slightly thickened. (Do not boil!)

Ladle the soup into warm soup plates, sprinkle with parsley, and serve with croutons, vegetables, and the remaining aïoli on the side.

Note: For a summer lunch or starter, serve the aïoli as a dipping sauce for a variety of raw vegetables, such as tomatoes, celery, sweet peppers, wax beans, baby carrots, and scallions. Accompany with hard-boiled eggs and boiled new potatoes.

Salad Niçoise

...

SERVES 6

FOR THE VINAIGRETTE

1/4 cup red-wine vinegar

1 tablespoon Dijon mustard

1 teaspoon dry mustard

Salt and freshly ground black pepper, to taste

3/4 cup olive oil

1 tablespoon chopped fresh herbs (any combination of chervil, parsley, chives, tarragon, and marjoram)

FOR THE SALAD

1 head oak leaf lettuce, washed and dried

1 head red leaf lettuce, washed and dried

1/4 pound green beans, stem-ends trimmed, cooked

1/4 pound yellow beans, stem-ends trimmed, cooked

24 cherry tomatoes

4 hard-boiled eggs, shelled and halved

12 cooked new potatoes, halved

1/2 small red onion, thinly sliced

2 (7-ounce) cans Italian-style tuna fish packed in oil, drained

2 tablespoons capers, washed and drained

8 oil-packed anchovy fillets, drained and patted dry

Prepare the vinaigrette: In a medium bowl, thoroughly whisk the vinegar, mustards, salt, and pepper. Gradually whisk in the oil until the vinaigrette is creamy. Stir in the herbs. Cover and refrigerate until ready to use.

Chill all the ingredients for the salad before combining.

Place all the ingredients, except the anchovies, in a large salad bowl and toss with enough vinaigrette to coat. Arrange the anchovy fillets on top of the salad or mash them into a paste and blend with the vinaigrette before tossing with the salad.

Grilled Duck Breast Salad

...

SERVES 4

1 head oak-leaf lettuce (or other loose-leaf lettuce)

1 cup shelled lima beans, fresh or frozen

4 (8 to 10 ounce) boneless duck breast halves (magrets)

1 teaspoon chopped fresh thyme leaves

Kosher salt and freshly ground black pepper, to taste

8 tablespoons olive oil

1 large yellow bell pepper, seeded, deveined, and cut into thin strips

2 medium red bell peppers, seeded, deveined, and cut into thin strips

2 tablespoons balsamic vinegar

1 tablespoon chopped fresh chervil

1 black truffle, cut into julienne (optional)

Wash and dry the lettuce and tear into bite-size pieces. Line a large plastic bag with a sheet of paper toweling. Add the greens and place another sheet on top of them. Close and refrigerate.

In a medium saucepan of lightly salted boiling water, cook the fresh lima beans for 10 to 15 minutes until tender. (If using frozen beans, cook for 1 to 2 minutes.) Drain, cool under cold water, and drain again. Set aside.

Rub the duck skin with the thyme. Season with salt and pepper, and set aside.

In a large skillet, heat 2 tablespoons of the oil over medium heat. Add the peppers and, tossing occasionally, cook until wilted, about 10 minutes, Using a slotted spoon, remove the peppers to a bowl and set aside.

Raise the heat to high. When the skillet begins to smoke, add the duck breasts, skin side down. Cook until the skin is golden, about 4 minutes. Turn and sear for 3 more minutes until the duck breasts are rare. (Magrets are best served rare; for medium rare, cook about 2 minutes longer.) Remove from the pan and reserve on a warm plate.

In a large bowl, whisk together the vinegar with salt and pepper to taste. Gradually whisk in the remaining 6 tablespoons oil. Add the greens and toss to coat. Divide the greens among 4 serving plates and sprinkle with the lima beans and pepper strips.

Slice the duck breasts across the grain into thin slices and arrange over the greens. Sprinkle with the chervil and optional truffle.

About Making Stock

Don't throw anything away!

Save all cooked chicken carcasses, raw wing tips, necks, and giblets (except the livers), and store in sealed plastic freezer bags and freeze. When you have stored up three or more carcasses, place them in a soup kettle with herbs, onions, celery and whatever soup vegetables you might have in the refrigerator—carrots, tomatoes, parsley stems, lettuce, leeks, or scallion ends. Cover with cold water and bring to a boil. Skim off any impurities that rise to the surface. Partially cover the pot and simmer over low heat for $1^1/_2$ hours. Strain the stock, discarding the solids. Return the stock to the stove and boil until reduced by half (or more depending upon the richness of stock you prefer.)

Cool the stock to room temperature, then refrigerate. It will be very gelatinous. Scoop into plastic freezer bags of various sizes according to your needs and freeze until needed.

Vegetable stocks can be made in the same fashion. Store all bits and pieces of onion, celery, carrots, turnips, parsley stems, mushroom stems, tomato skins, and other green noncruciferous vegetables in plastic bags in the vegetable bin of a refrigerator. When you have a good amount, wash the pieces, drain, boil the mixture with herbs and seasonings, strain, and reduce. Store in containers in the freezer.

Vegetables
and
Condiments

Wild Mushroom Bread Pudding

SERVES 6–8

1 pound (about 4^1/$_2$ cups) assorted wild mushrooms (preferably a
   combination of cremini, portabello, and porcini)

1^1/$_4$ cups rich chicken or turkey stock

1^1/$_4$ cups heavy cream

4 large eggs

1 cup milk

4 tablespoons (^{1}/$_2$ stick) unsalted butter

^{1}/$_4$ cup minced shallots

1 garlic clove, minced

1^1/$_2$ teaspoons chopped fresh thyme

Salt and freshly ground pepper, to taste

1 small loaf day-old brioche, crust removed, cut into ^{3}/$_4$-inch-thick
   slices and toasted

Clean the mushrooms with a mushroom brush or paper toweling. Cut off the stems and reserve. Slice the mushroom caps.

In a heavy saucepan, boil the stock and mushroom stems over medium heat until reduced by half, about 10 minutes. Add the heavy cream and cook until reduced to 1^1/$_2$ cups, about 15 minutes. Strain.

In a large bowl, whisk the eggs, then gradually whisk in the milk. Slowly whisk in the hot stock mixture and set aside.

In a large skillet, melt 3 tablespoons butter over medium-low heat. Add the shallots and garlic and sauté until translucent, about 5 minutes. Add the sliced mushrooms and thyme. Sauté until the mushrooms are lightly browned and their released liquid evaporates, about 10 minutes. Season with salt and pepper.

Use the remaining 1 tablespoon butter to lightly grease an 8^1/$_2$ x 14^1/$_2$-inch loaf pan.

Line the bottom with a layer of the toasted bread slices. Scoop in half of the mushroom mixture. Cover with another layer of brioche slices, then add the remaining mushroom mixture. Cover with third layer of brioche and slowly pour the egg mixture over all. Cover with plastic wrap and refrigerate overnight.

Preheat the oven to 350°F. Unwrap the loaf pan and press the bread down into the liquid. Cover the pan with aluminum foil and place in a roasting pan. Pour enough boiling water into the pan to come halfway up the sides of the loaf pan. Bake for about 2 hours until the pudding is set and the top is puffed and browned. (The pudding can be made ahead and reheated.) Cut into slices and serve warm.

Moroccan Eggplant with Tahini Yogurt

1 large eggplant
2 tablespoons olive oil
3 garlic cloves, chopped
2 ripe medium tomatoes, peeled, seeded, and chopped
$^1/_2$ roasted red bell pepper (see page 36), minced
Kosher salt and freshly ground pepper, to taste
2 tablespoons ground cumin
Juice of $^1/_2$ lemon

FOR THE YOGURT SAUCE

$^1/_2$ cup tahini paste
2 garlic cloves, minced
1 cup flat-leaf parsley leaves
$^3/_4$ cup plain yogurt
Juice of 2 lemons
Kosher salt, to taste

8 to 10 small pita breads

Preheat oven to 350°F.
Pierce the skin of the eggplant with a large kitchen fork. Place in an ovenproof dish and bake for 1 hour until the eggplant is tender and about to collapse. Slice the eggplant in half

lengthwise and allow to cool. Using a large spoon, scoop out the pulp, then chop it. (If excessively seedy, remove some of the seeds.) Set aside.

Heat the oil in a large nonreactive skillet over medium heat. Add the garlic and sauté until golden, about 1 minute. Add the tomatoes and roasted pepper. Season with salt and pepper. Bring to a simmer and cook for 10 minutes. Add the eggplant pulp and cumin. Cook an additional 20 minutes, stirring occasionally until most of the juice has evaporated but the mixture is still moist. Add the lemon juce and set aside.

Prepare the yogurt sauce: Pulse the tahini and garlic in a food processor until smooth. Add the remaining ingredients and pulse until blended.

To prepare the pitas, use scissors to carefully trim away the edges of each pita. Pull the two layers apart and cut each layer into 8 wedges. Toast wedges in a broiler or toaster oven. Serve the eggplant and sauce with the warm pita wedges and a variety of oil-cured olives. This dish can be served as a snack with drinks or as a first course.

Herbed Mashed Potatoes with Roquefort Cheese

SERVES 4–6

4 pounds russet or Idaho potatoes
1 cup milk
1/2 cup heavy cream
14 tablespoons (1 3/4 sticks) unsalted butter
Salt and freshly ground white pepper, to taste

2 to 3 gratings fresh nutmeg
1/4 cup mixed fresh herbs (any combination of parsley, chives, chervil, thyme, rosemary, or tarragon), chopped
8 ounces Roquefort cheese, crumbled

Peel and halve the potatoes and place in a kettle of lightly salted cold water to cover. Bring to a boil and cook until the potatoes are tender, or centers are easily pierced with a knife, about 15 minutes. Drain potatoes, return to the kettle, and cover.

In a medium saucepan, scald the milk and cream together over medium heat. Add the butter and continue cooking until the butter is melted. Do not let mixture boil over.

Push the potatoes through a ricer held over a large sauté pan; or mash them by hand in the kettle, using a potato masher. Stir the potatoes over medium heat and gradually pour in the scalded milk mixture. Mix until the potatoes are smooth and creamy.

Add the salt, pepper, and nutmeg and fold in the herbs. Serve potatoes on warm plates and sprinkle with Roquefort cheese. Serve with roasted chicken, grilled steak, or chops.

Note: Substitute soft goat cheese for the Roquefort (unseasoned, uncoated Montrachet is best). Cut the goat cheese into 1/4-inch rounds and place over each portion of mashed potatoes.

Corn Soufflé

Unsalted butter and flour for the soufflé pan
3 cups fresh corn kernels and the pulp from about 6 medium ears sweet corn (see Note)
1 cup milk
1 cup cream

3 tablespoons unsalted butter
3 tablespoons all-purpose flour
Large pinch ground mace
Salt and freshly ground black pepper, to taste
5 eggs, separated

Preheat the oven to 400°F. Butter a 3-quart shallow tin-lined pan or porcelain casserole dish and dust with flour. Shake out any excess.

Place the kernels and pulp in a food processor and pulse on and off until the kernels are lightly crushed. Set aside.

In a medium saucepan, combine the milk and cream and scald over medium heat.

In a medium saucepan, melt the butter. When the foam subsides, remove from the heat and whisk in the flour until smooth. Whisk in the cream mixture. Cook, whisking constantly, until the mixture thickens, about 5 minutes. Remove from the heat, fold in the crushed corn mixture, mace, and season with salt and pepper.

Using an electric mixer on high speed, beat the egg yolks for about 5 minutes until thick and lemon colored.

In a separate bowl, combine the egg whites with a pinch of salt. Beat the whites until they form stiff glossy peaks. Mix the yolks into the corn mixture, then fold in a large spoonful of the egg whites. Gently fold in the remaining whites. (Do not overblend; streaks of white should be visible.)

Pour the mixture into the prepared baking dish and bake for 15 minutes until puffed and lightly golden on top. Serve immediately.

Note: To prepare the corn, husk the ears and remove all of the silk. Using a sharp knife, cut away the kernels from the cob, slicing from the top of the ear downward and not too close to the cob. Place the kernels in a bowl. With a small spoon, scrape the pulp from the cobs into the bowl.

Ratatouille

...

SERVES 6–8

1 medium eggplant
1 teaspoon salt, plus more to taste
1 medium red bell pepper, cored, seeded, and deveined
1 medium yellow bell pepper, cored, seeded, and deveined
3 medium zucchini
1 cup olive oil
1 medium onion, chopped
3 garlic cloves, minced
2 large tomatoes, peeled, seeded, and chopped, or use 1 cup canned
   Italian-style tomatoes, drained

$^1/_2$ cup dry white wine
$^1/_2$ cup chicken stock, homemade or low-sodium canned
$^1/_2$ cup chopped basil
$^1/_2$ cup chopped fresh parsley
1 teaspoon chopped fresh mint
$^1/_2$ teaspoon chopped fresh thyme leaves
1 bay leaf
Freshly ground black pepper, to taste

Slice the eggplant into $^1/_4$-inch round slices. Stack the slices, a few at a time, and cut into $^1/_4$-inch dice. Place the eggplant in a colander and toss with 1 teaspoon salt. Set aside to drain.

Cut the peppers in $^1/_4$-inch strips and then into $^1/_4$-inch dice, and reserve. Cut the zucchini into $^1/_4$-inch slices, then $^1/_4$-inch strips, then $^1/_4$-inch dice. Reserve.

In a large deep nonreactive deep sauté pan, add $^1/_4$ cup of the olive oil and heat over medium heat. Add the onion and garlic and sauté for 10 minutes or until the onion is translucent. Add the tomatoes and cook until they release their juices, about 5 minutes. Transfer the mixture to a bowl and reserve.

Add about 2 tablespoons of the oil to the sauté pan and heat. Add the peppers and cook until they begin to lose some of their juice, about 5 minutes. Transfer the peppers to the bowl of vegetables and reserve.

Add another 2 tablespoons oil to the pan and heat. Add the zucchini and cook, tossing often for 5 minutes or until they become slightly limp.

Add the remaining $^1/_4$ cup of oil to the pan and heat. Squeeze the liquid out of the diced eggplant a fistful at a time. Add the eggplant to the pan. Cook, tossing often for 10 minutes until the eggplant becomes slightly limp.

Transfer the eggplant and any accompanying oil to another bowl and reserve. Add the wine and broth to the pan and bring to a boil. Reduce the heat and simmer for 5 minutes.

Add the reserved vegetable mixture and eggplant to the pan. Add the basil, parsley, mint, thyme, and bay leaf and season with salt and pepper. Cover slightly and simmer over medium-low heat for 30 minutes, stirring occasionally.

Drain the ratatouille in a colander set over a large bowl to catch the juices. Place the ratatouille and strained liquid in separate bowls and allow to cool to room temperature. Cover and refrigerate until chilled.

Spoon off the oil from the top of the ratatouille and save for another use. (It makes a delicious vinaigrette.) Add enough of the strained juice to moisten the ratatouille. Serve either as a first course or as an accompaniment to grilled meat or chicken.

Grilled Corn

12 ears fresh sweet corn
1 red hot chile pepper, seeded and deveined
1 teaspoon chopped fresh thyme leaves
1 teaspoon chopped cilantro leaves

2 garlic cloves, crushed
Salt and freshly ground black pepper, to taste
8 tablespoons (1 stick) unsalted butter or 1/4 cup olive oil

Build a charcoal fire in an outdoor grill. Pull off most of the corn husks, leaving only a double layer of husk attached. Remove and discard the silk.

Using a food processor fitted with the metal blade, pulse together all the ingredients, except the butter, until finely chopped. Add the butter and pulse until smooth.

Spread a light film of paste over the kernels and replace the attached husks.

When the coals are dusty and glowing, grill the corn, turning often, for about 10 minutes until the husks are lightly charred. Serve the corn in their husks.

Pickled Herring

1²⁄₃ cups salt

2 pounds herring fillets with skin, cut into 2-inch chunks (see Note)

3 cups distilled white vinegar

1 cup sugar

2 tablespoons pickling spices

1 green bell pepper, seeded, deveined, and chopped

1 red bell pepper, seeded, deveined, and chopped

1 medium white onion, sliced

1 medium red onion, sliced

2 tablespoons chopped fresh dill

In a large nonreactive soup pot, add the salt to 1 gallon of water. Stir well and allow to sit until the salt dissolves, stirring occasionally.

Rinse the fish fillets in cold water. Add the fillets to the salt brine and set aside for 45 minutes.

In a nonreactive medium saucepan, combine vinegar, sugar, and pickling spices. Bring to a boil over high heat, stirring until the sugar dissolves. Remove from the heat and set aside to cool completely.

When the pickling mixture is cool, add the red and green peppers, white and red onions, and the dill. Drain the herring completely and add to the mixture. Cover and refrigerate for 3 to 4 days, gently stirring occasionally.

Pack the herrings and vegetables in sterilized jars and fill with the pickling liquid. Cover and refrigerate. (Marinated fish will keep up to 3 weeks.)

Note: Blue herring is best for pickling. Mackerel or bluefish make good second choices. The pickling time depends on the thickness of the fish.

Hot Hot Tomato Chutney

...

MAKES ABOUT 5 PINTS

6 pounds (8 or 9 large) ripe tomatoes, cored and chopped

1/2 pound (2 medium) yellow onions, finely chopped

4 garlic cloves, minced

4 ounces fresh ginger, peeled and grated (about 1/2 cup)

3/4 cup sultana (golden) raisins

2 whole poblano chile peppers, seeded

1/4 cup Oriental hot red chili paste

1 tablespoon kosher salt, or to taste

2 tablespoons dark brown sugar

1 cup cider vinegar

Place all the ingredients except the brown sugar and vinegar in a large nonreactive stockpot and bring to a boil over high heat.

In a small nonreactive bowl, dissolve the sugar in the vinegar and stir into the kettle. Reduce the heat to low. Simmer, uncovered, stirring frequently to prevent scorching, until the chutney is the consistency of jam, about 1 1/2 hours or longer.

Remove the poblano chile peppers and discard. Ladle enough the hot chutney into sterilized pint jars to come within 1/8-inch of their tops. Wipe the rims and seal with the lids. Refrigerate after cooling. (Keeps for 4 to 6 weeks.)

Serve with meat loaf, cold meat dishes, and hamburgers.

Onion Marmalade

...

4 tablespoons (¹/2 stick) unsalted butter or vegetable oil
3 cups Vidalia or sweet red onions, thinly sliced
1 teaspoon granulated sugar
1 teaspoon kosher salt

¹/2 teaspoon white pepper
¹/2 cup rich chicken or vegetable stock, preferably homemade or
  low-sodium canned
¹/2 teaspoon chopped fresh thyme leaves, chopped or ¹/4 teaspoon dried

Heat the butter in a large skillet over medium heat. Add the onions, sugar, salt, and pepper. Cook until the onions turn a rich golden brown, stirring frequently to avoid sticking, about 15 minutes.

Add the broth and thyme and bring to a simmer, Immediately reduce the heat to low and cook, stirring frequently, for an additional 25 minutes or until the liquid reduces and the mixture is the consistency of thick jam.

Place the marmalade in a bowl and cool to room temperature. Cover and refrigerate. (If covered and refrigerated, the marmalade should keep about 2 weeks.)

Tapenade: Olive Paste

...

MAKES ABOUT 2 CUPS

2 cups Greek or Moroccan oil-cured olives

6 oil-packed anchovy fillets, drained and patted dry

2 tablespoons drained capers

2 tablespoons olive oil

1 tablespoon cognac

2 large garlic cloves, crushed

$^{1}/_{2}$ teaspoon grated lemon zest

$^{1}/_{8}$ teaspoon chopped fresh thyme leaves

$^{1}/_{8}$ teaspoon coarsely cracked black peppercorns

Place all the ingredients in a food processor fitted with the metal blade. Pulse on and off until the tapenade is grainy but not smooth. Place the mixture in a container, cover, and refrigerate. (If kept covered and refrigerated the tapenade should keep for up to 8 weeks, covered and refrigerated.)

Serve with cold vegetables, hard-boiled eggs, or as a sandwich enhancer.

FOR A MEDITERRANEAN SANDWICH

Spread two slices of crusty bread with tapenade. Layer one slice with arugula leaves, sliced mozzerella, and thinly sliced red onion.

Close, cut in half, and serve.

Pickled Pears

...

16 Kiefer or other hard winter pears, peeled, cored, and cut into
  $1/2$-inch-thick wedges
Juice of 1 lemon
4 cups cider vinegar
4 cups sugar
2 teaspoons pickling spices

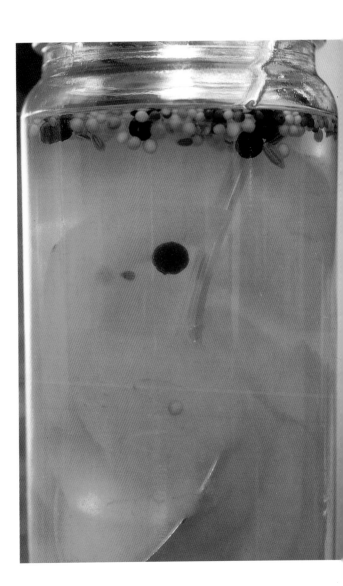

Slice the pears, dropping each slice immediately into a nonreactive bowl filled with the lemon juice to avoid discoloration.

In a heavy nonreactive soup pot, combine the pears with the remaining ingredients and 1 cup of cold water. Bring to a boil over high heat. Reduce the heat to low and simmer the pears for 45 minutes until almost tender.

Using a slotted spoon, transfer the pear wedges to sterilized jars. Divide the spices equally among the jars. Add enough of the syrup to reach $1/2$ inch from the jar rims. Wipe the rims and seal with the lids. Cool to room temperature. Store the pickled pears in the refrigerator. (Keeps 3 to 4 weeks.)

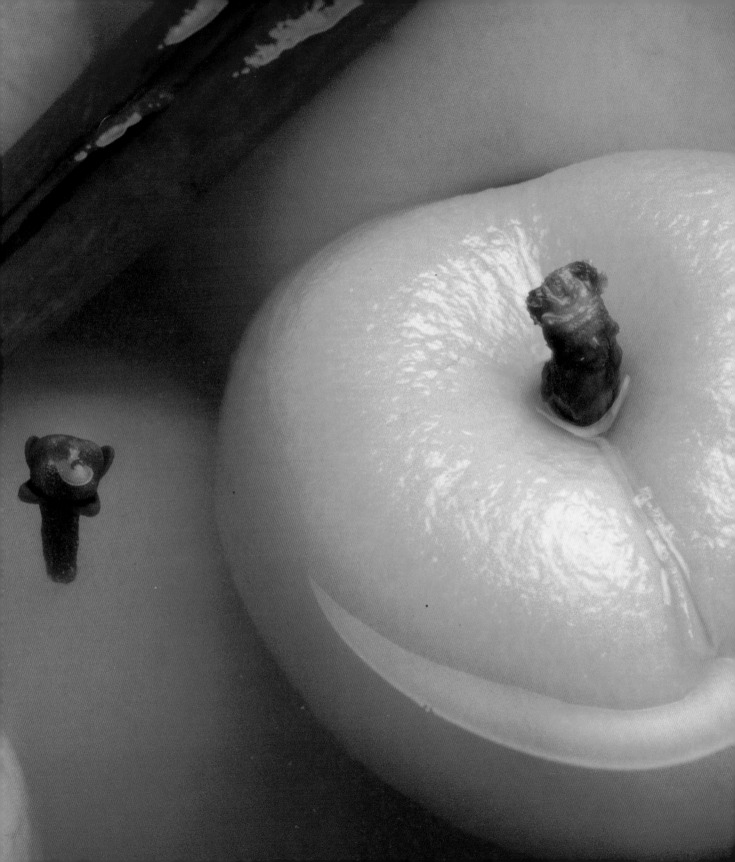

Plum Ketchup

1 quart (about 2 pounds) small, dark Italian plums, pitted and quartered
1/4 cup raspberry or other fruit vinegar
1-inch piece cinnamon stick

2 strips lemon zest, minced
1/4 teaspoon black peppercorns, crushed

In a medium nonreactive saucepan, bring all of the ingredients to a simmer over medium-low heat. Cook, stirring occasionally, for about 30 minutes until most of the juices evaporate and the ketchup is thick. Cool to room temperature. Store covered in the refrigerator. (The ketchup will keep 2 to 3 weeks.)

Serve as an accompaniment to to Shepherd's Pie (page 61), pork roasts, and chops.

Spiced Peaches

12 firm ripe peaches, well-washed to remove any fuzz
2 cups dark rum
2 cups sugar
1 cinnamon stick

3 star anise
1 tablespoon black peppercorns
1/4 teaspoon whole cloves
1/2 lemon, sliced

In large nonreactive kettle, combine the peaches and remaining ingredients with enough cold water to barely cover. Cover with a round of waxed paper. Bring to a boil over high heat. Reduce the heat to low and simmer until the peaches can be easily pierced with a sharp paring knife, about 15 minutes.

Transfer the peaches to a shallow dish, leaving the syrup in the saucepan. When the peaches are cool enough to handle, peel them and return the peels to the saucepan. Raise the heat to medium and cook the syrup until it is reduced by half.

Divide the peaches into 2 (1-quart) canning jars. Strain the hot syrup, then ladle over the peaches. Divide the spices equally and discard the peels and lemon slices. Cover with the lids to seal and cool to room temperature. When cooled, tighten the lids and store the peaches in the refrigerator. (The peaches will keep for 4 to 5 weeks.)

Serve with roast loin of pork, roast fresh or smoked ham, or as a dessert.

Desserts
and
Drinks

Orange Brûlée

FOR THE CANDIED ZEST AND ORANGES
3 large Seville or tart oranges
¹/₂ cup sugar
¹/₂ cup grenadine syrup

FOR THE CUSTARD
2 cups heavy cream
6 large egg yolks
¹/₄ cup sugar
1 tablespoon Grand Marnier or other orange-flavored liqueur

Prepare the zest: Using a sharp paring knife or vegetable peeler, remove the zest from the orange in long wide strips, avoiding as much of the white pith as possible. Store the peeled oranges in a plastic bag and refrigerate. Cut the zest into fine, needle-thin julienne.

In a medium-heavy saucepan, combine the sugar and grenadine and ¹/₂ cup cold water and bring to a boil over medium heat. Boil for 5 minutes. Stir in the orange julienne and simmer for 5 minutes, stirring occasionally with a wooden spoon. Transfer the zest and syrup to a bowl and cool, then cover and refrigerate until ready to use.

Prepare the oranges: With a sharp knife, carefully cut away the pith and membranes from the oranges' exteriors. Using a paring knife, carefully cut out the sections from the inner membranes. Arrange the sections on a shallow plate, cover, and refrigerate until ready to use.

Prepare the custard: In a small saucepan, heat the cream just until it begins to steam. Remove from the heat. In a medium heatproof bowl (stainless steel works well), whisk the egg yolks with the sugar until thick and lemon colored. Fit the bowl on top of a medium saucepan of simmering water. Whisk vigorously, gradually adding the Grand Marnier. As the mixture begins to thicken, slowly whisk in the hot cream. When it is thick enough to coat the whisk, about 2 minutes, remove the mixture from the heat and pour into another bowl.

Divide the orange sections among four (about 1 cup) shallow heatproof bowls or ceramic crème brûlée dishes. Pour the custard around the orange sections, not on top. One by one, place each plate under a hot broiler for 15 seconds, or long enough for the custard to glaze.

Remove some of the grenadine zest from the syrup and sprinkle on top of each serving.

Chocolate-Brittle Ice Cream

...

FOR THE ICE-CREAM CUSTARD

5 ounces bittersweet chocolate, finely chopped

2 tablespoons unsalted butter

1/4 cup brewed espresso coffee, cold or at room temperature

2 cups heavy cream

2 cups milk

2/3 cup sugar

1 star anise

1/2 vanilla bean, split, seeds scraped out and reserved

5 egg yolks

FOR THE BRITTLE

1 cup sugar

1 cup slivered almonds

1/4 cup dark rum

Prepare the ice-cream custard: In a medium saucepan, melt the chocolate with the butter over low heat. Stir in the espresso and set aside.

In a medium saucepan, combine the heavy cream, milk, sugar, star anise, and the vanilla bean with its scraped seeds. Over medium heat, cook the mixture until it steams. Remove from the heat.

In a large bowl, whisk the egg yolks until lemon colored. Slowly whisk in the hot milk mixture. Return to the saucepan and whisk constantly over low heat until the custard begins to thicken, about 10 minutes.

Whisk a little of the custard into the melted chocolate to warm it. Pour chocolate mixture into the custard and whisk to combine. Set the pan in a bowl of ice and stir until cool.

Cover and refrigerate until chilled, about 1 hour.

Prepare the brittle: In a small saucepan, combine the sugar with 1/2 cup water. Bring to a boil, stirring to dissolve the sugar. Reduce the heat and cook without stirring until the sugar begins to caramelize and turn amber, about 3 minutes. Add the slivered almonds and swirl to combine. Pour mixture onto a lightly oiled baking sheet and cool until firm. Break the brittle into small bits pieces.

When the custard is chilled, remove the star anise and vanilla bean. Add the brittle to the mixture and stir in the rum. Freeze in an ice-cream maker according to the manufacturer's directions. Transfer the ice cream to a covered container and freeze for at least 2 hours before serving.

Cherry Clafouti

9 tablespoons (1 stick plus 1 tablespoon) unsalted butter
3 eggs
¾ cup sugar
¾ cup all-purpose flour, sifted

½ teaspoon vanilla extract
1 pound Bing or Queen Anne cherries, stemmed and pitted
2 cups heavy cream, lightly whipped

Preheat the oven to 350°F. Coat a 10-inch round glass or porcelain pie pan evenly with 1 tablespoon of the butter. Melt the remaining 8 tablespoons butter in a small saucepan over low heat and reserve.

Using an electric mixer set at high speed, beat the eggs with the sugar until the mixture is thickened and a light lemon color, about 3 minutes. Add the flour and vanilla and mix until thoroughly blended. Set aside for 15 minutes.

Arrange the cherries over the bottom of the buttered pie pan. Pour the batter evenly over the cherries. Bake for 45 minutes until golden and puffy. Serve at room temperature with the whipped cream.

Note: You can substitute sliced green gage or red plums for the cherries.

Roasted Pineapple Caribe

1 large ripe pineapple
1/2 cup sugar
1/2 cup dark rum
1/2 vanilla bean, split, seeds scraped out and reserved

1 (2-inch) cinnamon stick
1/2 cup honey
Vanilla or cinnamon ice cream, for serving

Preheat the oven to 375°F.
Pare away and discard the pineapple skin. Cut pineapple lengthwise into quarters and cut away the core. Set aside.

In a deep ovenproof skillet, combine the sugar, rum, vanilla bean and seeds, and cinnamon stick over medium heat. Warm the mixture, stirring often, until the sugar melts. Cook about 5 minutes until the mixture to thickens slightly, then add the honey and stir until melted. Add the pineapple quarters, coat with the mixture, and simmer for 5 minutes.

Transfer the skillet to the oven and bake, basting with the liquid once or twice, for about 25 minutes or until the mixture darkens and caramelizes.

Remove the pan from the oven. On a carving board, cut the pineapple into thin slices. Fan out the slices on the side of serving plates and drizzle with the sauce. Serve with a scoop of vanilla or cinnamon ice cream set next to the pineapple.

Spiced Poached Figs with Pinot Noir Syrup

SERVES 4

FOR THE SYRUP
3 cups pinot noir or other robust red wine
1 cup cold water
1 cup sugar
12 whole black peppercorns
3 whole cloves

1 (2-inch) cinnamon stick
1 sprig fresh thyme

16 large firm ripe figs
Crème Anglaise (page 111)

Prepare the syrup: In a nonreactive saucepan, combine all the ingredients except the figs and Crème Anglaise and bring to a boil over high heat. Reduce the heat to low and simmer for 10 minutes. Cool.

Reheat the mixture to a simmer, add the figs, and poach for 4 to 5 minutes until they begin to puff up. Using a slotted spoon, transfer the figs to a shallow baking pan and let cool.

Place syrup back over high heat and simmer vigorously over high heat for about 30 minutes until reduced to 1 cup.

Cool.

Serve the figs with the syrup and accompanied by Crème Anglaise.

Note: To poach pears, peel 4 firm ripe pears, add to the simmering syrup, and poach for 20 minutes or until the pears can easily be pierced with a sharp paring knife. Remove the pears and reduce the syrup as directed.

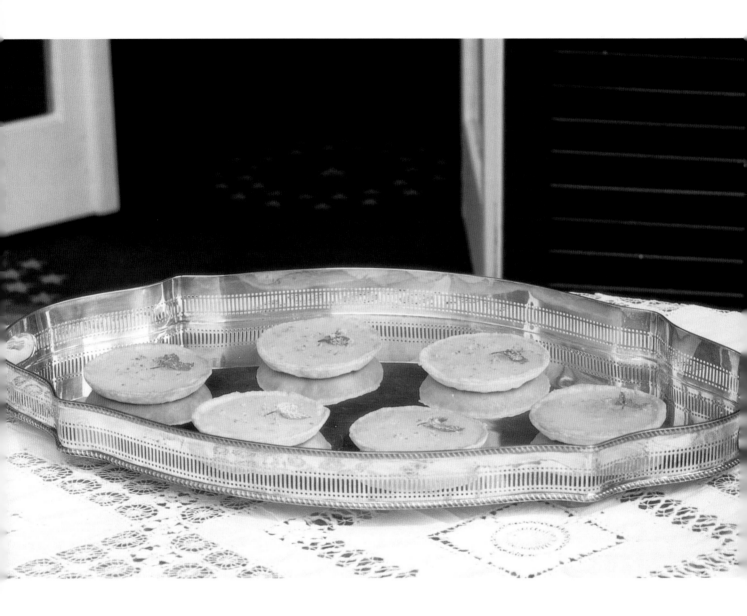

Lemon Curd Tartlets

Tart Dough Recipe (see page 116)

FOR THE CURD
½ cup lemon juice, strained

1 ½ teaspoons arrowroot
8 egg yolks
½ cup sugar
2 tablespoons unsalted butter, chilled, cut into bits

Prepare the tart dough recipe according to directions. Form dough into a ball, then cut into bits. Place half of the dough in the refrigerator and allow to rest for about 30 minutes; freeze the other half for another use.

Quickly roll out the dough on a lightly floured surface to ⅛-inch thickness or less. Using a cookie cutter, shape the dough into rounds to fit 6 (3½-inch) tartlet molds. Press each round into a mold and prick the bottoms and sides with the tines of a small fork or poultry needle. Set the shells on a baking pan, cover with plastic wrap, and refrigerate for 30 minutes or longer.

Preheat oven to 375°F.

Cut out rounds of lightweight foil a little larger than the diameter of the shells. Lightly butter the shiny sides of the foil and place butter-side-down against the shells. Add a teaspoon of rice or small, uncooked beans. Place pan on center rack of oven and bake for 10 minutes, or until pastry is still soft and bubbles up. Remove the foil, prick the shells again, and continue to bake another 3 or 4 minutes until lightly golden. Allow to cool 10 minutes before unmolding onto a rack.

Prepare the curd: Place the lemon juice, 1 cup cold water, and sugar in a medium saucepan and bring to a boil over high heat. In a small bowl, dissolve the arrowroot in ½ cup cold water. Whisk in the yolks until the mixture is smooth and lemon colored. Slowly pour 1 cup of the lemon mixture in the yolk mixture and whisk thoroughly. Pour the mixture back into the saucepan and bring to a simmer and whisk for 10 minutes or until thick. Remove the mixture and whisk in the butter bits. Scrape into a bowl and cover with plastic wrap. Puncture the plastic wrap in 2 or 3 places to allow the heat to escape. Cool completely.

When ready to serve, whisk the curd lightly and spoon into the shells. Makes 6 individual shells.

Coconut Flan

FOR THE CARAMEL
3/4 cups granulated sugar

FOR THE CUSTARD
1 1/2 cups grated fresh or packaged unsweetened (desiccated) coconut

3 cups milk
1/2 cup sugar
3 whole eggs
6 egg yolks

In a heavy saucepan combine the sugar with 2 tablespoons cold water and let stand until moistened. Over medium heat, swirl the pan continuously until the sugar dissolves. When the syrup becomes a medium-dark amber color, pour the caramel into the bottom of a 2-quart shallow baking dish. Immediately lift the mold using dry kitchen towels (the mold will be hot), and turn and tilt it until the bottom and sides are coated with caramel. Set aside.

Prepare the custard: Preheat the oven to 325°F. Spread the coconut on a baking sheet. Bake, stirring once or twice until toasted and golden brown, about 5 to 10 minutes, Set aside.

In a medium saucepan, bring the milk, sugar, and coconut to a simmer over medium heat, stirring often to dissolve the sugar. Remove from the heat and steep for 20 minutes.

Using an electric mixer set at high speed, beat together the whole eggs and egg yolks until thick and lemon colored, about

1 minute. Strain the coconut-milk mixture through a fine sieve pressing down to extract the milk from the coconut. Discard the coconut. Gradually beat into the egg mixture.

Pour the custard into the caramelized dish. Place within a larger roasting pan and add enough boiling water to come halfway up the sides of the pan. Place on center rack of the oven and bake for about 50 minutes or until the custard is set, but wobbly when shaken. (A paring knife inserted in the center of the custard will come out clean but slightly wet.)

Remove the custard from the water bath and cool for 20 minutes. Cover and refrigerate for at least 3 hours or overnight.

To serve, run the blade of a paring knife around the edges of the dish. Dip the dish in a roasting pan filled with hot water for a minute or two. Set a large deep serving platter that can hold the caramel sauce over the dish. Hold tightly, invert, and unmold.

Ovos Nevados

...

FOR THE CRÈME ANGLAISE
1 quart milk
1 vanilla bean, split, seeds scraped out and reserved
8 egg yolks
2/3 cup sugar

FOR THE MERINGUE
2/3 cup egg whites (about 5 whites)
1/4 teaspoon cream of tartar

1 pinch of salt
1/2 cup sugar

FOR THE CARAMEL
1/2 cup sugar
2 tablespoons water

Grated zest of 1 lime

Prepare the crème anglaise: In a heavy bottomed saucepan, heat the milk and vanilla bean and its seeds over medium heat until steaming. Remove from the heat and set aside. In a medium heatproof bowl that will snugly fit on top of a saucepan (or in the top of a double boiler), whisk the egg yolks and sugar until thick and lemon colored. Gradually whisk in the hot milk.

Set the bowl over a medium saucepan of simmering water, stirring constantly with a wooden spoon until it thickens enough to coat the spoon, 7 to 8 minutes. Remove from the heat. Set a fine-mesh sieve over a bowl and strain the custard, discarding the vanilla bean. Cool for 20 minutes, then cover and chill.

For the meringue: In a large shallow saucepan, heat 2 inches of water to 170°F and keep constant at that temperature (just under a simmer).

In the bowl of a standing electric mixer, beat the egg whites with the cream of tartar and salt at low speed until they foam. Gradually increase the speed to high, while adding the sugar. Beat until the whites form stiff shiny peaks.

Using a large serving spoon, form egg shapes and gently push the meringues into the hot water, leaving room for them to expand as they poach. Poach for 3 to 4 minutes. Carefully turn them over with a slotted spoon and poach for another 3 to 4 minutes until set. Lift out the meringues using a slotted spoon and place on a wire baking rack lined with a kitchen towel made of thin linen or cotton. Repeat until all the meringue is used. (They will keep for several hours.)

When ready to serve, pour the chilled sauce into a shallow serving dish and float the meringues on top.

Prepare the caramel: In a heavy saucepan combine the sugar and 2 tablespoons water and let stand until moistened. Over medium heat, swirl the pan until the sugar dissolves. Continue to cook until the syrup turns a golden amber color.

Using the tines of a fork, form thin strands of syrup and drizzle them over the meringues. Sprinkle the surface with the lime zest and serve.

Lemon Cake

SERVES 8–10

FOR THE CAKE
1 box Duncan-Hines Lemon Supreme Cake Mix
1 ($3^1/2$ ounce) box Jello Instant Lemon Pudding
$^1/_4$ cup fresh lemon juice
4 eggs
$^1/_2$ teaspoon lemon extract
$^2/_3$ cup canola oil

FOR THE GLAZE
1 cup plus 2 tablespoons confectioners' sugar
$^1/_4$ cup fresh lemon juice
1 teaspoon grated lemon zest
$^1/_2$ teaspoon lemon extract

Fresh berries and Crème Anglaise (page 111), for serving

Preheat the oven to 350°F. Lightly butter a 10-cup Bundt or fluted tube pan. In a medium bowl combine the cake mix and instant pudding and set aside.

In a large glass measuring cup, combine the lemon juice and enough cold water to make $^2/_3$ cup of liquid. Add to the dry ingredients along with the eggs and lemon extract and mix on low speed. Pour in the oil and beat at medium speed until the mixture is smooth.

Pour mixture into the prepared pan. Bake for 45 minutes or until the top is golden and the cake is springy to the touch.

Prepare the glaze: In a small bowl, whisk the 1 cup confectioners' sugar, lemon juice, zest, and lemon extract until smooth. Set aside.

Cool the cake for 5 minutes. Unmold onto a plate. Using a poultry needle or toothpick, pierce 1-inch-deep holes into the top of the cake. Slowly spoon the glaze over the cake and cool completely. When ready to serve, dust with the remaining 2 tablespoons confectioner's sugar and serve with fresh berries and Crème Anglaise.

Berry Shortcake

FOR THE SYRUP
$^1\!/_2$ *cup sugar*
$^1\!/_2$ *cup mint leaves*

FOR THE SHORTCAKE
2 cups all-purpose flour
1 tablespoon sugar
1 tablespoon baking powder

1 teaspoon salt
5 tablespoons unsalted butter, chilled and cut into small bits
1 cup heavy cream

FOR THE FILLING
3 pints strawberries or combination of strawberries, raspberries, and blackberries
$^1\!/_2$ *pint heavy cream, whipped*

Prepare the syrup: In a heavy small saucepan, bring the sugar and 1 cup cold water to a boil over high heat, stirring with a wooden spoon until the sugar dissolves. Continue to boil, without stirring, for 5 minutes, then remove from the heat. Crush the mint leaves and add to the syrup. Cool completely, then strain and discard the mint leaves.

Prepare the shortcake: Preheat the oven to 350°F. In a large bowl, sift together the flour, sugar, baking powder, and salt. Using your fingers, work the butter into the flour mixture until it looks crumbly.

Stir in the cream and mix just until it is absorbed and the dough is no longer sticky and releases from the sides of the bowl.

On a lightly floured surface, flatten the dough into a 1-inch flat cake. Cut into 8 equal wedges. Form each wedge into 1-inch-thick rounds. Place the shortcakes on an ungreased baking sheet. Bake for 25 to 35 minutes until golden.

Prepare the berries: Wash, hull, and slice the strawberries, then place in a bowl and add the other berries, if using. Add as much of the mint-infused syrup as you like and toss. Let stand for 10 minutes.

Using a serrated knife, cut the shortcakes in half crosswise and place them on individual serving plates. Divide the berries onto the bottom half, replace the tops, and serve with the whipped cream.

Plum Tart

...

FOR THE TART DOUGH
1¹/₂ cups all-purpose flour, sifted
¹/₂ cup cake flour (not self-rising)
1 tablespoon sugar
¹/₂ teaspoon salt
8 tablespoons (1 stick) unsalted butter, chilled and cut into bits
1 tablespoon vegetable shortening, chilled

¹/₂ cup ice water

About 24 dark Italian plums (or 10 red plums), pitted and sliced
2 tablespoons sugar
Whipped cream or vanilla ice cream, for serving

Preheat the oven to 425°F.
Prepare the tart dough: Sift the flours, sugar, and salt into the bowl of an electric mixer fitted with the paddle attachment. On low speed, add the butter, bit by bit, and shortening and mix until the mixture is the consistency of fine cornmeal. Increase the speed to medium and slowly add the cold water, beating just until the dough forms a ball and pulls away from the sides of the bowl. Do not overmix. If the pastry is too dry, beat in a few drops of water on low speed. Turn the dough out onto a cool lightly floured surface. Smear the pastry on the surface with the heel of your hand for a final blending and form into a thick flat cake. Wrap the dough in plastic wrap and refrigerate until just chilled, about 20 minutes.

On a lightly floured surface, rapidly roll out the dough into a rectangle approximately ¹/₈-inch thick and to fit a large flat baking sheet. Cover with plastic wrap and refrigerate for 30 minutes. Cover the pastry with the plum slices in rows, overlapping them slightly and leaving 1-inch border. Fold the rim of the pastry up to, and slightly overlapping, the plums. Dust the plums with 1 tablespoon of the sugar. Bake for 20 to 30 minutes until the crust is browned. Dust with the remaining 1 tablespoon sugar. Serve with whipped cream or ice cream.

Note: Sliced tart apples can be substituted for the plums.

Bread Pudding Soufflé with Whiskey Sauce

SERVES 8

FOR THE SOUFFLÉ
Unsalted butter and sugar, for the mold

4 eggs, separated

1 cup sugar

1 teaspoon vanilla extract

$1/4$ teaspoon ground cinnamon

$1/4$ teaspoon freshly grated nutmeg

4 cups milk

5 cups day-old French bread with crust (from a large loaf, not a thin baguette), cut into 1-inch cubes

Pinch of salt

$1/2$ cup sultana (golden) raisins, soaked in enough dark rum to cover

$1/2$ cup chopped pecans

FOR THE SAUCE
1 cup heavy cream

2 egg yolks

2 tablespoons sugar

$1/4$ cup bourbon

Prepare the soufflé: Preheat the oven to 350°F. Butter and sugar an 8-cup soufflé dish, tapping out excess sugar.

In a medium bowl, whisk the egg yolks with $3/4$ cup of the sugar, vanilla, cinnamon, nutmeg until thick, creamy and lemon colored. Whisk in the milk.

Place the cubed bread in a large bowl. Pour the milk mixture over the bread. Set aside for 45 minutes, so the bread soaks up the milk mixture.

Using an electric mixer at low speed, beat the egg whites until they are foamy. Add the salt and increase the speed to medium. When the whites begin to form stiff peaks, gradually add the remaining $1/4$ cup of sugar, increasing the speed to high. Beat until the whites are stiff and glossy.

Stir the raisins and pecans into the soaked bread. Fold in the meringue, making sure not to overmix. Transfer the mixture into the prepared mold and bake for 35 to 40 minutes until puffed and golden.

Prepare the sauce: In a double boiler, heat the cream over simmering water. In a medium bowl, whisk the egg yolks with the sugar until lemon colored. Gradually whisk in the heated cream.

Return the mixture to the double boiler and cook over simmering water, stirring constantly until thick enough to coat the back of a wooden spoon. Slowly add the bourbon.

Pour the sauce into a heated sauceboat and serve with the soufflé.

Tropical Fruit Sorbet

...

About 18 passion fruit (enough to yield 1 cup juice) or substitute 1 cup
  defrosted frozen purée (available in Hispanic markets)
2 cups orange juice, strained

1 cup Simple Syrup (page 123)
1 tablespoon vodka

Halve the passion fruits and scoop out the pulp with the seeds. Using the metal blade of a food processor, add the pulp and pulse on and off 2 or 3 times. (Be careful, overpulsing will darken the pulp.) Pour the pulp into a fine wire strainer set over a bowl. Press down on the mixture with a rubber spatula and discard the seeds.

Combine the passion fruit juice, orange juice, and simple syrup. Taste for sweetness, adding more syrup as needed. Cover and refrigerate until chilled.

Pour the vodka into the bottom of a prechilled container of an electric ice-cream maker. (The vodka helps keep the sorbet smooth and discourages it from sticking to the bottom of the container.) Pour in the fruit mixture. Freeze the sorbet according to the manufacturer's directions.

Note: To make other fruit sorbets (such as mango, papaya, guava, berry, or pineapple), peel the fruit as needed and purée the pulp. If the fruits have seeds, purée and strain the pulp. , Add 1 to 1½ cups Simple Syrup to 3 cups pulp depending on the sweetness of the fruit. Follow the remaining instructions

Blueberry Breakfast Muffins

2 tablespoons unsalted butter, for the muffin tins
2 cups all-purpose flour
1 cup blueberries
$1/3$ cup granulated sugar
1 tablespoon baking powder
1 teaspoon salt

1 cup buttermilk
2 eggs, beaten
2 tablespoons unsalted butter, melted
1 teaspoon grated lemon zest
1 teaspoon vanilla extract

Preheat the oven to 400°F. Butter a muffin tin and set aside. In a small bowl, toss $1/4$ cup of the flour with the blueberries and set aside. In a large mixing bowl, combine the remaining $1^3/4$ cups flour, sugar, baking powder, and salt. Using a wooden spoon, blend in the buttermilk, eggs, and melted butter.

Fold in the lemon zest and vanilla and mix just until smooth. Gently fold in the blueberries. Fill the muffin cups two-thirds full.

Bake for 20 minutes, or until golden brown. Cool on a wire rack for 2 to 3 minutes before removing from the pan. Serve the muffins warm.

Lemonade

...

MAKES ABOUT 6 SERVINGS

FOR THE SIMPLE SYRUP
4 cups water
2 cups sugar

3 cups fresh lemon juice (about 12 large lemons), strained
3 cups club soda or ice water
Mint sprigs, for serving

Prepare the simple syrup: Place the water and sugar in a medium saucepan and bring to a boil over high heat, stirring with a wooden spoon until the sugar dissolves. Boil without stirring for 5 minutes. Cool to room temperature. Cover and refrigerate. (Refrigerated, the syrup will keep for 3 to 4 weeks.)

In a large pitcher, combine $1\frac{1}{2}$ cups of the lemon juice with 1 cup simple syrup and 3 cups cold water. Mix and pour into ice-cube trays and freeze.

When ready to serve, combine the remaining $1\frac{1}{2}$ cups lemon juice, 1 cup simple syrup and 3 cups soda water in a pitcher and mix. Pour over tall glasses filled with the lemonade ice cubes. Add a mint sprig to each and serve.

Note: For other fruit flavors, such as strawberry, raspberry, pineapple, and watermelon, combine 1 cup strained pulp, 1 cup simple syrup, and 3 cups cold water. Freeze in the ice-cube tray. Use as ice cubes for the lemonade.

Moroccan Mint Tea

...

MAKES ABOUT 6 SERVINGS

Brew a pot of loose orange-pekoe or black tea leaves. Fill glasses with fresh mint sprigs, and pour the tea over the mint. Add sugar to taste.

Index

...

Appetizers, 14
    Artichokes Benedict, 14, *15*
    Black Bean Soup, 34, *34*
    Bruschetta with Fresh Tomatoes, *22, 23*
    Cannellini Beans and Tuna, 23
    Caprese Salad, 30, *30*
    Celery-Root Remoulade, 26
    Cold Oysters and Lamb Sausage, 24
    Country Salad, 25, *25*
    Fish Soup with Rouille, 36
    Littlenecks with Herb Butter, 18
    Papaya with Shrimp and Yogurt-Dill Dressing, 31, *31*
    Pistou: Mediterranean Vegetable Soup with Basil Sauce, 32, *33*
    Puff Pastry with Asparagus and Mushrooms, *16, 17*
    Purée of Pea Soup with Mint, 35, *35*
    Steamed Mussel and Potato Salad, *20,* 21
    Succotash and Lobster, 27
    Summer Salad, 28, 29, *29*
Artichokes Benedict, 14
Bahia Fish Stew (see Moqueca, 64)
Berry Shortcake, *114,* 115
Black Bean Soup, 34, *34*
Blueberry Breakfast Muffins, 120, *121*
Bourride with Aïoli, *70,* 71
Braised Lamb Shanks with White Beans, 52
Bread Pudding Soufflé with Whiskey Sauce, 117
Bruschetta with Fresh Tomatoes, *22, 23*
Cannellini Beans and Tuna, 23
Caprese Salad, 30, 30
Celery-Root Remoulade, 26
Cherry Clafouti, 101
Chicken Pot Pie, *48,* 49
Chocolate Brittle Ice Cream, 100
Choucroute, 57
Coconut Flan, 108, *109*
Cold Oysters and Lamb Sausage, 24, *24*

Condiments, 87
    Hot Hot Tomato Chutney, *88, 89*
    Onion Marmalade, 90, *91*
    Pickled Herring, 87, *87*
    Pickled Pears, 93, *93*
    Plum Ketchup, 95
    Spiced Peaches, *94,* 95
    Tapenade, 92, *92*
Corn Soufflé, 82, *83*
Country Salad, 25, *25*
Crab and Salmon Cakes, 68, *69*
Desserts, 98
    Berry Shortcake, *114,* 115
    Blueberry Breakfast Muffins, 120, *121*
    Bread Pudding Soufflé with Whiskey Sauce, 117
    Cherry Clafouti, 101
    Chocolate-Brittle Ice Cream, 100
    Coconut Flan, 108, *109*
    Lemon Cake, 112, *113*
    Lemon Curd Tartlets, *106,* 107
    Orange Brulée, 98
    Ovos Nevados, *110,* 111
    Plum Tart, 116, *116*
    Roasted Pineapple Caribe, *102, 103*
    Spiced Poached Figs with Pinot Noir Syrup, 104
    Tropical Fruit Sorbet, *118,* 119
Drinks, 123
    Lemonade, *122,* 123
    Moroccon Mint Tea, 123, *123*
Fish Soup with Rouille, 36–37, *37*
Grilled Corn, 86, *86*
Grilled Duck Breast Salad, 74
Grilled Swordfish with Salt Crust and Gin-Lime Butter, 62, 63
Herbed Mashed Potatoes with Roquefort Cheese, 81
Hot Hot Tomato Chutney, *88, 89*
Lamb Stew, 53

Lemon Cake, 112, *113*
Lemon Curd Tartlets, *106*, 107
Lemon Risotto, *44*, 45
Lemonade, *122*, 123
Littlenecks with Herb Butter, 18
Main Courses, 41
    About Making Stock, 75
    Bourride with Aïoli, *70*, 71
    Braised Lamb Shanks with White Beans, 52
    Chicken Pot Pie, *48*, 49
    Choucroute, 57
    Crab and Salmon Cakes, 68, *69*
    Grilled Duck Breast Salad, 74
    Grilled Swordfish with Salt Crust and Gin-Lime Butter, *62*, 63
    Lamb Stew, 53
    Lemon Risotto, *44*, 45
    Marinated Grilled Salmon, 60, *61*
    Meatloaf, 56
    Moqueca: Bahia Fish Stew, 64, *65*
    Osso Buco, 51, *51*
    Pasta with Clams, Mussels and Sausage, 42, *43*
    Pumpkin Baked with Creamed Shrimp, Rio Style, *66*, 67
    Red Scallop Pasta, *40*, 41
    Roast Chicken, 50
    Salad Niçoise, *72*, 73
    Shepherd's Pie, *58*, 59
    Steak Salad with Vegetables, 54, *55*
    Stewed Apples with Macaroni and Cheese, 46, *47*
Marinated Grilled Salmon, 60, *61*
Meatloaf, 56
Mediterranean Vegetable Soup with Basil Sauce (Pistou), 32, *33*
Moqueca: Bahia Fish Stew 64, *65*
Moroccan Eggplant with Tahini Yogurt, 80, *80*
Moroccan Mint Tea, 123, *123*
Olive Paste (Tapenade), 92
Onion Marmalade, 90, *91*

Orange Brulée, 98
Osso Buco, 51, *51*
Ovos Nevados, *110*, 111,
Papaya with Shrimp and Yogurt-Dill Dressing, 31, *31*
Pasta with Clams, Mussels, and Sausage, 42, *43*
Pickled Herring, 87, *87*
Pickled Pears, 93
Pistou: Mediterranean Vegetable Soup with Basil Sauce, 32, *33*
Plum Ketchup, 95
Plum Tart, 116, *116*
Puff Pastry with Asparagus and Mushrooms, *16*, 17
Pumpkin Baked with Creamed Shrimp, Rio Style, *66*, 67
Purée of Pea Soup with Mint, 35, *35*
Ratatouille, *84*, 85
Red Scallop Pasta, *40*, 41
Roast Chicken, 50
Roasted Pineapple Caribe, *102*, 103
Salad Niçoise, *72*, 73
Shepherd's Pie, *58*, 59
Spiced Peaches, *94*, 95
Spiced Poached Figs with Pinot Noir Syrup, 104, *105*
Steak Salad with Vegetables, 54, *55*
Steamed Mussel and Potato Salad, *20*, 21
Stewed Apples with Macaroni and Cheese, 46, *47*
Stock, 75
Succotash and Lobster, 27
Summer Salad, *28*, 29, *29*
Tapenade: Olive Paste, 92
Tropical Fruit Sorbet, *118*, 119
Vegetables, 78
    Corn Soufflé, 82
    Grilled Corn, 86
    Herbed Mashed Potatoes with Roquefort Cheese, 81
    Moroccan Eggplant with Tahini Yogurt, 80
    Ratatouille, 85
    Wild Mushroom Bread Pudding, 78